KNOWLEDGE   ...URE

KNOWLEDGE AND ITS
PLACE IN NATURE

Hilary Kornblith

CLARENDON PRESS · OXFORD

OXFORD
UNIVERSITY PRESS

Great Clarendon Street, Oxford OX2 6DP

Oxford University Press is a department of the University of Oxford.
It furthers the University's objective of excellence in research, scholarship,
and education by publishing worldwide in

Oxford New York

Auckland Cape Town Dar es Salaam Hong Kong Karachi
Kuala Lumpur Madrid Melbourne Mexico City Nairobi
New Delhi Shanghai Taipei Toronto

With offices in

Argentina Austria Brazil Chile Czech Republic France Greece
Guatemala Hungary Italy Japan South Korea Poland Portugal
Singapore Switzerland Thailand Turkey Ukraine Vietnam

Oxford is a registered trade mark of Oxford University Press
in the UK and in certain other countries

Published in the United States
By Oxford University Press Inc., New York

British Library Cataloguing in Publication Data

Data available

Library of Congress Cataloging in Publication Data

Data available

ISBN 0-19-924631-9
ISBN 0-19-924632-7 (Pbk.)

1 3 5 7 9 10 8 6 4 2

Printed in Great Britain by Biddles Ltd., King's Lynn, Norfolk

To Robin

ACKNOWLEDGEMENTS

MY work on this book began as a result of a conversation with Brian McLaughlin at Rutgers University a number of years ago. I casually mentioned that I thought of knowledge as a natural kind, and McLaughlin spent the next hour or so asking me a series of questions that served to focus a very large body of previously inchoate thought. I returned home and promptly sat down to put those thoughts on paper. The result, which was published as 'Knowledge in Humans and Other Animals', became the outline for this book. It is a pleasure to be able to acknowledge my indebtedness to McLaughlin here.

That I also owe a large debt to Alvin Goldman will be obvious to anyone who reads this book or knows any of my previously published work. Although much of my discussion of Goldman below focuses on areas of disagreement, there are far larger areas of agreement between us, not the least of which involves my use of his reliability account of knowledge. There is a large personal debt here as well. My friendship with Alvin Goldman goes back more than twenty years now, and during that period I have been the benificiary of regular discussion, comment, criticism, and constant encouragement.

Conversations over the years with Laurence BonJour, Robert Brandom, Richard Feldman, Mark Kaplan, Jonathan Vogel, and Michael Williams have been tremendously helpful, as have the many opportunities to present the ideas in this book before various departmental colloquia. In my own department, ideas were constantly tried out long before they were fit to present in public, and the constructive help from David Christensen, William Mann, and Derk Pereboom were invaluable. Christensen and Pereboom both read the entire manuscript of the book and provided me with detailed feedback that resulted in numerous changes. Philip Robbins, who also read the entire manuscript, provided me with much helpful criticism. I feel especially fortunate to have had the benefit of Colin Allen's reading of the manuscript, which resulted in countless changes and additions. Two anonymous readers for Oxford University Press gave the book a very careful reading, and their suggestions have done much to improve it. The thoroughly constructive and sympathetic suggestions I received from Oxford's readers were especially appreciated since neither of them was, to put it mildly, entirely convinced by the main theme of the book; indeed, one reader remarked that he or she disagreed with almost everything I said. Peter Momtchiloff of Oxford University Press has been a wonderful editor. His confidence in this project from the earliest stages has been very much appreciated.

As my work on this book progressed, I came to recognize the extent to which many of the ideas contained here were not entirely original to me. Aside from the debts already acknowledged, it is important to point out that Ruth Millikan's work has much in common with this book and shows ways of developing these ideas which I have not pursued. The same may be said of work by Henry Plotkin and Peter Godfrey-Smith. There is also a deep affinity with some of Fred Dretske's work.

A number of pieces of this book have previously appeared in print. Chapter 1 is reprinted, with substantial revisions and additions, from 'The Role of Intuition in Philosophical Inquiry', in M. DePaul and W. Ramsey (eds.), *Rethinking Intuition* (Rowman & Littlefield, 1998), 129–41. Portions of Ch. 2 appeared as part of 'Knowledge in Humans and Other Animals', *Philosophical Perspectives*, 13 (1999), 327–46; it is reprinted by permission of Blackwell Publishers. Sections of Ch. 4 appeared in 'Introspection and

Misdirection', *Australasian Journal of Philosophy*, 67 (1989), 410–22, and are reprinted here by permission of Oxford University Press. That chapter also includes portions of 'The Unattainability of Coherence', which appeared in J. Bender (ed.), *The Current State of the Coherence Theory* (Kluwer, 1989), 207–14. Much of Ch. 5 appeared as 'Epistemic Normativity', in *Synthese*, 94 (1993), 357–76 (published by Kluwer), while a small part of it is taken from 'Knowledge in Humans and Other Animals'. Permission of these publishers to reprint is gratefully acknowledged.

CONTENTS

I

Investigating Knowledge Itself

NOT so long ago, philosophy was widely understood to consist in an investigation of our concepts. There were books with titles such as *The Concept of Mind*;[1] *The Concept of a Person*;[2] *The Concept of Law*;[3] *The Concept of Evidence*;[4] and *The Concept of Knowledge*.[5] The idea that philosophy consists in, or, at a minimum, must begin with an understanding and investigation of our concepts is, I believe, both natural and very attractive. It is also, I believe, deeply mistaken. On my view, the subject matter of ethics is the right and the good, not our concepts of them. The subject matter of philosophy of mind is the mind itself, not our concept of it. And the subject matter of epistemology is knowledge itself, not our concept of knowledge. In this book, I attempt to explain what knowledge is.

My insistence that epistemology should not concern itself with our concept of knowledge requires that I depart, in important ways,

---

[1] Gilbert Ryle, *The Concept of Mind* (Barnes & Noble, 1949).

[2] A. J. Ayer, *The Concept of a Person and Other Essays* (Macmillan, 1964).

[3] H. L. A. Hart, *The Concept of Law* (Oxford University Press, 1961).

[4] Peter Achinstein, *The Concept of Evidence* (Oxford University Press, 1983).

[5] Panayot Butchvarov, *The Concept of Knowledge* (Northwestern University Press, 1970).

from some common practices. I will not, for the most part, be comparing my account of knowledge with my intuitions about various imaginary cases; I will not be considering whether we would be inclined to say that someone does or does not have knowledge in various circumstances. I do not believe that our intuitions, or our inclinations to say various things, should carry a great deal of weight in philosophical matters. But if we abandon these traditional philosophical tools, then how are we to proceed? How are we to go about investigating knowledge itself, rather than our concept of knowledge? Indeed, what could it even mean to suggest that there is such a thing as knowledge itself apart from our concept of it?

In this chapter, I focus on issues of method. Conceptual analysis, the use of imaginary examples and counterexamples, and appeals to intuition are the stock-in-trade of many philosophers. Indeed, George Bealer[6] has described the appeal to intuitions as part of 'the standard justificatory procedure' in philosophy, and, as a simple sociological matter, I believe that Bealer is right; appeals to intuition are standard procedure. More than this, Bealer detects the use of this standard procedure in philosophers who otherwise differ on a wide range of issues; even philosophers who favor a naturalistic epistemology, Bealer argues, make use of appeals to intuition.[7] This is a special problem for naturalists, as Bealer sees it, because naturalists are committed to an epistemology that makes no room for appeals to intuition. So much the worse, Bealer argues, for naturalism. The very practice of philosophy is incompatible with a naturalistic epistemology.

---

[6] See George Bealer, 'The Philosophical Limits of Scientific Essentialism', *Philosophical Perspectives*, 1 (1987), 289–365; 'The Incoherence of Empiricism', in S. Wagner and R. Warner (eds.), *Naturalism: A Critical Appraisal* (Notre Dame University Press, 1993), 163–96; and 'Intuition and the Autonomy of Philosophy', in M. DePaul and W. Ramsey (eds.), *Rethinking Intuition: The Psychology of Intuition and Its Role in Philosophical Inquiry* (Rowman & Littlefield, 1998), 201–39. Page numbers in parentheses refer to 'The Incoherence of Empiricism'.

[7] See also Frank Jackson, *From Metaphysics to Ethics: A Defense of Conceptual Analysis* (Oxford University Press, 1998), p. vii: 'And, as you might expect, if I am right about our need for it, conceptual analysis is very widely practiced—though not under the name of conceptual analysis. There is a lot of "closet" conceptual analysis going on.'

Now the kind of epistemology I favor, and the kind I will argue for here, is a form of naturalism, and Bealer's argument is thus directly relevant to the conduct of this enquiry. If Bealer is right, a naturalistic epistemology is self-undermining. Bealer is not the only one to have made this sort of argument. Similar arguments have been made by Laurence BonJour,[8] Frank Jackson,[9] Mark Kaplan,[10] and Harvey Siegel.[11] Naturalistic epistemology, on this view, proclaims allegiance to a theory that is fundamentally at odds with the philosophical practice of its adherents. A naturalistic epistemology is thereby shown to be untenable.

The clarity and force with which Bealer and others have presented this argument requires that it be given a fair hearing. A naturalistic epistemology has far greater resources, I will argue, than these philosophers have given it credit for. In the course of responding to this argument, I hope to explain how it is that philosophical theorizing may flourish while assigning a significantly smaller role to appeals to intuition than do the critics of naturalism. And in providing an account of philosophical theory construction from a naturalistic point of view, I hope to explain how it is that one may reasonably hope to give an account of knowledge itself, and not just the concept of knowledge.

1.1 Appeals to intuition: The phenomenon

First, let us get clear about the phenomenon. Although any characterization of the phenomenon will be highly contentious, there is no difficulty in giving examples of the practice at issue. We will thus do

---

[8] Laurence BonJour, 'Against Naturalistic Epistemology', *Midwest Studies in Philosophy*, 19 (1994), 283–300, and *In Defense of Pure Reason* (Cambridge University Press, 1998). [9] Frank Jackson, *From Metaphysics to Ethics*.
[10] Mark Kaplan, 'Epistemology Denatured', *Midwest Studies in Philosophy*, 19 (1994), 350–65.
[11] Harvey Siegel, 'Empirical Psychology, Naturalized Epistemology and First Philosophy', *Philosophy of Science*, 51 (1984), 667–76.

best to pin down the practice by way of examples, examples of what we hereby dub 'appeals to intuition'; later we may address the question of what it is these examples are examples of.

There are substantial bodies of literature in philosophy that are driven in large part by frankly acknowledged appeals to intuition and are motivated by a desire to formulate accounts that square with those intuitions. Thus, in epistemology, there is the literature on the analyses of knowledge and justification, and especially would-be solutions to the Gettier problem. Imaginary cases are described, involving Brown and his travels in Spain; Nogot, Havit, and their vehicles; Tom Grabit and his kleptomaniacal proclivities at the library; gypsy lawyers; Norman the clairvoyant; barn façades in the countryside; and a host of others. In each of the cases described, there is a good deal of agreement about whether, under the described conditions, a subject knows, or is justified in believing, something to be the case. Intuitions about these cases are then used to clarify the conditions under which various epistemic notions rightly apply. No empirical investigation is called for, it seems. Each of us can just tell, immediately and without investigation of any kind, whether the case described involves knowledge, or justified belief, or neither.

But epistemologists are not the only ones to use this method. In philosophy of language, there is the literature on the Gricean account of meaning, replete with subjects and their self-referential intentions, including the American soldier who hopes to convince his Italian captors that he is German by uttering the one German sentence he knows, 'Kennst du das Land wo die Zitronen bluhen?'; not to mention a character who intends to clear a room with his rendition of 'Moon Over Miami', at least in part, of course, in virtue of his audience recognizing that very intention. Here we have quite clear intuitions about when it is that a subject means something by an utterance, and when a subject merely means to achieve a certain effect without meaning anything by the utterance at all. There is also the literature on the causal or historical theory of reference, with the cases of Gödel, Schmidt, and the goings-on on Twin Earth.

There is the literature on personal identity, with its cases of brain transplantation, memory loss, and duplication. And there is the literature in moral philosophy involving children who amuse themselves by pouring gasoline on cats and igniting them; the woman who wakes up one morning to find herself an essential part of the life-support system for an ailing violinist; and a very large number of people unaccountably loitering on trolley tracks.

This method of appeal to intuitions about cases has been used in every area of philosophy, and it has often been used with subtlety and sophistication. There are those—and I count myself among them—who believe that there are substantial limitations to this method, and that some of these bodies of literature have diverted attention from more important issues. Even we, however, must acknowledge not only that the method of appeal to intuitions plays an important role in actual philosophical practice, but also that it has been used to achieve some substantial insights in a wide range of fields. We need an account of how it is that this method may achieve such results.

1.2 Bealer's account of intuition and the standard justificatory procedure

Now George Bealer offers us precisely such an account, and he uses this account to argue that naturalism[12] is self-defeating. In order to see how Bealer's argument proceeds, we must begin with his characterization of the phenomenon.

---

[12] Bealer has argued against a number of different targets, including naturalism, scientific essentialism, and empiricism. There are, of course, numerous versions of each of these views, and one may consistently subscribe to more than one of them. Indeed, the view I favor, and that I defend here, may rightly be described as falling under each of these three headings. It is for this reason that I feel called upon to answer Bealer's attacks on all these positions.

Bealer describes what he calls 'the standard justificatory procedure' (pp. 164–7). As Bealer notes, 'we standardly use various items—for example, experiences, observations, testimony—as *prima facie* evidence for things, such as beliefs and theories' (p. 164). After describing a typical Gettier example, Bealer notes that intuitions as well count as prima facie evidence. But what are intuitions? According to Bealer, 'When we speak of intuition, we mean "*a priori* intuition"' (p. 165).

Although use of the term 'intuition' varies widely among philosophers, Bealer is careful to make his use of the term clear. 'Intuition', Bealer tells us, 'must . . . be distinguished from common sense . . . common sense is an amalgamation of various widely shared, more or less useful empirical beliefs, practical wisdom, *a priori* intuitions, and physical intuitions. Common sense certainly cannot be *identified* with *a priori* intuition' (p. 167). This distinction, Bealer tells us, is 'obvious once [it] is pointed out' (ibid.).

Once this account of the standard justificatory procedure is in place, with its reliance on intuition in Bealer's sense,[13] the route to an indictment of naturalism is clear. Naturalists subscribe to a principle of empiricism: 'A person's experiences and/or observations comprise the person's *prima facie* evidence' (p. 163). This rules out intuition as a legitimate source of evidence, and thus flies in the face of the standard justificatory procedure. Naturalists themselves make use of intuitions; they too subscribe, in practice, to the standard justificatory procedure. So naturalistic theory is belied by naturalistic practice. Indeed, if consistently followed in practice, Bealer argues, naturalistic theory would not only rule out philosophy generally as illegitimate, but, given the role intuition plays in 'following rules and procedures—for example, rules of inference' (p. 167), a

---

[13] I don't mean to suggest that Bealer's usage here is idiosyncratic; it isn't. Compare, for example, BonJour's notion of intuition: 'judgments and convictions that, though considered and reflective, are not arrived at via an explicit discursive process and thus are (hopefully) uncontaminated by theoretical or dialectical considerations' (*In Defense of Pure Reason*, 102).

consistent naturalist would have little room left for legitimate belief of any sort at all.

Bealer argues that some naturalists face an additional problem as well. Those who wish to make use of, rather than eliminate, epistemic terminology will find, Bealer argues, that their theory is at odds with their practice in yet another way. What Bealer calls 'the principle of naturalism' holds that 'the natural sciences . . . constitute the simplest comprehensive theory that explains all, or most, of a person's experiences and/or observations' (p. 163). Naturalists also endorse what Bealer calls 'the principle of holism': 'A theory is justified . . . for a person if and only if it is, or belongs to, the simplest comprehensive theory that explains all, or most, of the person's prima facie evidence' (ibid.). When these two principles are added to the principle of empiricism, which limits our source of prima-facie evidence to observation, naturalists are forced to eschew all epistemic terminology, because 'the familiar terms "justified," "simplest," "theory," "explain," and "prima facie evidence" . . . do not belong to the primitive vocabulary of the simplest regimented formulation of the natural sciences' (p. 180). Not only is naturalistic theory at odds with naturalistic practice, but the very terms in which naturalistic theory is formulated, Bealer argues, are disallowed as illegitimate by that very theory. Naturalism is thus found to be self-defeating twice over.

There is more to naturalism, I believe, than is to be found in Bealer's account of it. There is room within a naturalistic epistemology for the practice of appeals to intuition, suitably understood, and also for the use of epistemic terminology. What I wish to do is explain how the naturalist may accommodate these phenomena. Much of what I say will be familiar; the story I have to tell, I believe, is at least implicit in the work of a number of investigators working within the naturalistic tradition.[14] But in squarely addressing these

[14] For example, Michael Devitt remarks, in a footnote to his 'The Methodology of Naturalistic Semantics,' *Journal of Philosophy*, 91 (1994), 545–72: 'The naturalist does not deny "armchair" intuitions a role in philosophy but denies that their role has to be seen

charges against naturalistic epistemology, we may not only put them to rest, but we may also lay the foundation for a deeper understanding of proper method in philosophical theorizing.

1.3 A naturalistic account of appeals to intuition

Naturalists and their opponents have divergent views about how philosophy ought to be practiced. At the same time, however, there is a great deal more agreement in actual practice than there is in theory about that practice. I do not believe that these differences are insignificant, and later in this chapter I will want to say something about what those differences are and why they matter. But for now, I want to focus on the areas of agreement in practice between naturalists and anti-naturalists, and I will assume that the characterization Bealer gives of the standard justificatory procedure accurately characterizes that common practice. That is, I will assume, with Bealer, that philosophers of all sorts assign prima-facie weight to experience, observation, testimony, *and intuition*, although I will not assume, with Bealer, that intuition here comes down to 'a priori intuition'. Instead, I will take intuition to be pinned down by the paradigmatic examples of it given above in sect. 1.1.

How should naturalists regard the standard justificatory procedure? The first thing to say about the intuitions to which philosophers appeal is that they are not idiosyncratic; they are widely shared, and—to a first approximation—must be so, if they are to do any philosophical work. Some philosophers will say, 'I'm just trying

as a priori: the intuitions reflect an empirically based expertise at identification' (564 n. 27). Devitt refers there to Bealer's work. The present chapter may be seen as an attempt to expand on this remark of Devitt's. After completing a draft of this chapter, my attention was drawn to the work of Terry Horgan which has many points of contact with the views expressed here. See Horgan's 'The Austere Ideology of Folk Psychology', *Mind and Language*, 8 (1993), 282–97, and Terence Horgan and George Graham, 'Southern Fundamentalism and the End of Philosophy', *Philosophical Issues*, 5 (1994), 219–47. Finally, see also Richard Boyd's 'How to Be a Moral Realist', in Geoffrey Sayre-McCord (ed.), *Essays on Moral Realism*, esp. pp. 192–3.

to figure out what *I* should believe; I'm just trying to get my own intuitions into reflective equilibrium.' But even philosophers who say this sort of thing must recognize that wholly idiosyncratic intuitions should play no role even in figuring out what they themselves ought to believe. If I attempt to offer a philosophical account of knowledge by drawing on my intuitions, and it should turn out that crucial intuitions upon which my account relies are had by no one but me, then this will not only dramatically reduce the interest of my account for others; it ought, as well, reduce the interest of my account for me. If my intuitions are wildly idiosyncratic, then most likely the project of accommodating them is no longer one that is engaged with the phenomenon others are attempting to characterize. Unless I can show that others have been somehow misled, what I ought to conclude is that I am probably the one who has been misled, and I ought to focus my attention on correcting my own errors, rather than taking my intuitive judgments at face value. The intuitions of the majority are not definitive, but they do carry substantial epistemic weight, at least in comparison with the intuitions of any single individual, even oneself.

Why is it that the intuitions of the majority carry such weight? It is not, of course, that we merely wish to be engaged in the project, whatever it may be, that other philosophers are engaged in. This would make philosophy into a shallow enterprise, a kind of intellectual imitation game in which the participants seek to engage one another in what they are doing, without any regard for what that might be. Instead, we must be assuming that disagreement with the majority is some evidence of error, and now the question is how that error should be characterized.

Now it is at this point that many philosophers will be tempted to bring in talk of concepts and conceptual analysis: in appealing to our intuitions, it will be said, we come to understand the boundaries of our shared concepts. But I don't think this way of seeing things is illuminating. By bringing in talk of concepts at this point in an epistemological investigation, we only succeed in changing the subject:

instead of talking about knowledge, we end up talking about our concept of knowledge.

As I see it, epistemologists should be trying to understand what knowledge is. There is a robust phenomenon of human knowledge, and a presupposition of the field of epistemology is that cases of knowledge have a good deal of theoretical unity to them; they are not merely some gerrymandered kind, united by nothing more than our willingness to regard them as a kind. More than this, if epistemology is to be as worthy of our attention as most epistemologists believe, and if knowledge is to be as worthy of our pursuit, then certain deflationary accounts of knowledge had better turn out to be mistaken. What I have in mind here is those social constructivist accounts which, while granting a substantial theoretical unity to cases of knowledge, see that unity as residing in the social role that knowledge plays. Knowledge, on this kind of view, is merely a vehicle of power. Knowledge may well play some such social role, but its ability to play such a role, if I am right, is explained by a deeper fact, and it is this deeper fact about knowledge that gives it its theoretical unity.[15]

Now one of the jobs of epistemology, as I see it, is to come to an understanding of this natural phenomenon, human knowledge. Understanding what knowledge is, if the project turns out as I expect it will, will also, simultaneously, help to explain why knowledge is worthy of pursuit. When we appeal to our intuitions about knowledge, we make salient certain instances of the phenomenon that need to be accounted for, and that these are genuine instances of knowledge is simply obvious, at least if our examples are well chosen. What we are doing, as I see it, is much like the rock collector who gathers samples of some interesting kind of stone for the purpose of figuring out what it is that the samples have in common.

[15] I have discussed this point at greater length in 'A Conservative Approach to Social Epistemology', in Fred Schmitt (ed.), *Socializing Epistemology* (Rowman & Littlefield, 1994), 93–110, and in 'Naturalistic Epistemology and Its Critics', *Philosophical Topics*, 23 (1995), 237–55.

We begin, often enough, with obvious cases, even if we do not yet understand what it is that provides the theoretical unity to the kind we wish to examine. Understanding what that theoretical unity is is the object of our study, and it is to be found by careful examination of the phenomenon, that is, something outside of us, not our concept of the phenomenon, something inside of us. In short, I see the investigation of knowledge, and philosophical investigation generally, on the model of investigations of natural kinds.

This point is quite important, for what it means is that a good deal of the work involved in defining the subject matter under investigation is actually done by the world itself rather than the investigator. The subject matter of the rock collector's investigation is the natural kind, whatever it may be, which (most of) the samples picked out are members of; but the investigator need not be in a position to characterize the essential features of that kind. The investigator's concept of that kind, therefore, because it may be quite incomplete or inaccurate, need not itself do very much of the work of defining the subject matter under study.

This is contrary, of course, to what defenders of conceptual analysis claim. Frank Jackson, for example, nicely lays out the traditional view about the importance of concepts in defining subject matter.

The role of intuitions about possible cases so distinctive of conceptual analysis is precisely to make explicit our implicit folk theory and, in particular, to make explicit which properties are really central to [the subject matter under study]. For surely it *is* possible to change the subject, and how else could one do it other than by abandoning what is most central to defining one's subject? Would a better way of changing the subject be to abandon what is *less* central?[16]

But surely a central point in favor of the causal or historical theory of reference is the observation that reference may remain stable even in the face of substantial changes in belief. It is not that subject matter is changed, as Jackson rhetorically suggests, by changing less

[16] Jackson, *From Metaphysics to Ethics*, 38.

central rather than more central defining features, for what is central or peripheral to our concept plays little role in defining subject matter in the first place. Rather, subject matter is defined by way of connections with real kinds in the world, and what we regard as central or defining features does not determine the reference of our terms.

When philosophical investigation is viewed on the model of the investigation of natural kinds, the method of appeal to intuitions is, I believe, easily accommodated within a naturalistic framework. The examples that prompt our intuitions are merely obvious cases of the phenomenon under study. That they are obvious, and thus uncontroversial, is shown by the wide agreement that these examples command. This may give the resulting judgments the appearance of a priority, especially in light of the hypothetical manner in which the examples are typically presented. But on the account I favor, these judgments are no more a priori than the rock collector's judgment that if he were to find a rock meeting certain conditions, it would (or would not) count as a sample of a given kind.[17] All such judgments, however obvious, are a posteriori, and we may view the appeal to intuition in philosophical cases in a similar manner.[18]

[17] What of the claim that something is a natural kind? Is that too known empirically? I believe that it is. Consider, again, the case of gold. What caught our attention and resulted in the introduction of the term, let us suppose, was a collection of salient features such as the color, reflectance pattern, malleability, and so on of a number of samples of rock. It was an empirical discovery that these constituted a natural kind, i.e. that these samples were not, from a theoretical perspective, merely heterogeneous, but rather that they shared some deep, underlying properties responsible for the more superficial properties that initially attracted our attention. The same is true of natural-kind terms generally. While a person introducing a term may well believe, at the time the term is introduced, that the referent of the term is a natural kind, subsequent investigation may reveal that this belief is false. By the same token, a term may be introduced for a property that is, in fact, a natural kind, without the person introducing the term recognizing that fact.

[18] Here I simply take for granted a causal or historical account of the reference of natural-kind terms. While the details of such a theory remain to be established, the general outline is, I believe, perfectly clear in the foundational work of Kripke and Putnam. The following points should be agreed upon by all sides: (1) The initial

What should we say about the rock collector's judgments at early stages of investigation, i.e. prior to any deep theoretical understanding of the features that make his samples samples of a given kind? Such judgments are, of course, corrigible, and they will change with the progress of theory. What seemed to be a clear case of a given kind in the absence of theoretical understanding may come to be a paradigm case of some different kind once the phenomena are better understood. At the same time, it would be a mistake to see these initial naïve judgments as wholly independent of background theory. Our rock collector is naïve, but he is not a tabula rasa. Background knowledge will play a substantial role in determining a first-pass categorization of samples. Judgments about which features of the rocks are even deemed relevant in classification—hardness, for example, but not size perhaps—are themselves theory-mediated, although the operation of theory here is unselfconscious and is better revealed by patterns of salience than it is by overt appeal to principle. The extent to which naïve investigators agree in their classifications is not evidence that these judgments somehow bypass background empirical belief, but rather that background theory may be widely shared.

So too, I want to say, with appeals to intuition in philosophy. These judgments are corrigible and theory-mediated. The extent of agreement among subjects on intuitive judgments is to be explained by common knowledge, or at least common belief, and the ways in which such background belief will inevitably influence intuitive judgment, although unavailable to introspection, are none the less quite real.

samples that prompt the introduction of a natural-kind term need not all be members of the kind in order for reference to occur; (2) The most central beliefs about a kind held by early investigators may turn out to be false without thereby undermining reference. These points are not so much argued in the text as taken for granted. What I do argue is that reference to knowledge may work in precisely the same way as reference to, for example, gold, and that there are no problems specific to the case of knowledge beyond those already addressed in the work on more paradigmatic natural kinds.

Indeed, I want to push this analogy considerably further. The judgments of rock collectors at early stages of investigation are substantially inferior, epistemically speaking, to those at later stages, when theoretical understanding is further advanced. We should not say that initial judgments are of no evidential value, for were this the case progress in theory would be impossible. Our untutored judgment must have some purchase on the phenomenon under investigation; but, that said, it must also be acknowledged that judgment guided by accurate background theory is far superior to the intuitions of the naïve. Intuition must be taken seriously in the absence of substantial theoretical understanding, but once such theoretical understanding begins to take shape, prior intuitive judgments carry little weight unless they have been endorsed by the progress of theory. The greater one's theoretical understanding, the less weight one may assign to untutored judgment.

All this applies equally well to the case of appeals to intuition in philosophy. We sometimes hear philosophers speak of some intuitions as 'merely' driven by theory, and thus to be ignored. While it is certainly true that judgments driven by bad theories are not to be taken seriously, the solution is not to try to return to some pure state of theory-independent judgment, before the fall, as it were; rather the solution is to get a better theory. Intuition in the absence of theory does not count for nothing, especially if no credible theory is available. But this is not to award high marks to intuitive judgment before the arrival of successful theory, let alone after, when the initially low value of such judgment drops still lower.

Now if this account is correct, why do philosophers spend so much time scrutinizing their intuitions, that is, looking inward, if, on my view, what they are really interested in is external phenomena? I have two things to say about this. First, if I am asked a question about rocks, for example, one way to answer the question is to ask myself what I believe the answer is. Although I am asked a question about rocks, I answer it by enquiring into what I believe. This is a perfectly reasonable thing to do if I have good reason to think that my current beliefs are accurate, or if I do not have access to a better source of information. By looking inward, I answer a question about an external phenomenon. This, to my mind, is what we do when we consult our intuitions.

At the same time, however, I do not think that this can be the whole story here, and this is where the difference between the practice of naturalists and that of anti-naturalists comes into play. If my account is correct, then what we ought to be doing is not just consulting the beliefs we already have, but more directly examining the external phenomena; only then would appeals to intuition be given what, on my view, is their proper weight. Thus, appeal to intuition early on in philosophical investigation should give way to more straightforwardly empirical investigations of external phenomena. This is, to my mind, just what we see in the practice of naturalistically minded philosophers. Just a few decades ago, the philosophical practice of naturalistically minded epistemologists, for example, was almost indistinguishable from that of their more traditionally minded colleagues. Examples and counterexamples were used to motivate various accounts of knowledge and justification, and the progress of these accounts was shepherded along by a succession of appeals to intuition. This was, by my lights, a good thing to do at that stage of the investigation. Important insights were gained, which, given the absence of available explicitly articulated theory, could not have been gained by any other means. But now, as theory has progressed, more straightforwardly empirical investigation should be called upon; and this, of course, is just what we see. There is work on the psychology of inference, concept formation, cognitive development, and so on. Similarly, at the social level there is work on the distribution of cognitive effort, and, more generally, the social structures of science that underwrite and make scientific knowledge possible. As theory has advanced here, raw appeals to intuition have declined. Just look at the difference between early papers by Fred Dretske and Alvin Goldman, for example, and their more recent work. Similar results may be found by looking at naturalistically minded work in philosophy of mind, and even in ethics, where work in cognitive science and anthropology have been shaping the work of contemporary naturalists. The difference in methodology between naturalists and their more traditional colleagues has, to my mind, been paying substantial dividends for those willing to draw on empirical work. But even those who disagree with me here will have to agree that naturalistic methodology is now importantly different from that of other philosophers, even if not very long ago it would have been difficult to separate the naturalists from the non-naturalists by looking at their methods.

From a naturalistic perspective, there are substantial advantages to looking outward at the phenomena under investigation rather than inward at our intuitions about them. Most obviously, since it is some external phenomenon that we are interested in, we should approach it by the most direct means possible, rather than the more indirect approach of looking at what we currently believe about it. Aside from being indirect, the approach of examining our intuitions clearly robs us of the best available source of correctives for current mistakes. Moreover, the appeal to imaginable cases and what we are inclined to say about them is both overly narrow and overly broad in its focus. It is overly narrow because serious empirical investigation of a phenomenon will often reveal possibilities which we would not, and sometimes could not, have imagined before. It is overly broad because many imaginable cases are not genuine possibilities and need not be accounted for by our theories. We might be able to imagine a rock with a certain combination of color, hardness, malleability, and so on, and such a rock, were it to exist, might be difficult or impossible to fit into our current taxonomy. But this raises no problem at all for our taxonomic principles if the imagined combination of properties is nomologically impossible. On the naturalistic view, the same may be said for testing our philosophical views against merely imaginable cases.

The suggestion that our intuitions about knowledge might actually be mistaken in the ways in which our intuitions about, say, gold can be will strike some philosophers as implausible. It is important, however, to realize that our intuitions about knowledge are, in important ways, historically conditioned. Descartes's idea that knowledge required certainty was surely a product of his view that things firm and lasting in the sciences could only be achieved if scientific claims could be given an absolute guarantee. As it turned out, Descartes was wrong about this. In ways Descartes could never have anticipated, the sciences have gone on to achieve levels of ever-increasing explanatory and predictive success coupled with technological applications crucially dependent upon the approximate truth of their theoretical claims. These successes, producing things 'firm and lasting in the sciences', of just the sort Descartes hoped to achieve, did not depend in any way on the sort of certainty Descartes took to be a prerequisite for knowledge. The view that knowledge requires certainty is no longer widely held; it is an intuition that very few people have any more. In retrospect, this change in people's intuitions about the relationship between knowledge and certainty can be seen as a byproduct of the ways in which scientific success has actually been achieved. It is now just obvious to almost everyone that knowledge is possible without certainty. But it would be a mistake to see this realization as a matter of a priori insight into the nature of knowledge. Properly understood, it is, however indirectly, a claim empirically justified by the manner in which knowledge has in fact been gained.

Now all of this would make little difference if our intuitions responded to relevant empirical evidence in a timely fashion. Consulting our intuitions would be just as accurate as looking directly at the relevant phenomena if only our intuitions were suitably responsive to appropriate evidence. But there is no reason to think that our intuitions are suitably responsive to available evidence. Changing a society's intuitions about a particular subject matter takes a good deal of time. It is one thing for the scientific community to make an important discovery; quite another for that discovery to become common knowledge. It takes still longer before our whole conception of a phenomenon comes to seem so obvious that we can no longer even remember what it was like to conceive of it in another way. But if we take the long historical view, this is exactly what happens with our intuitions when important discoveries are made. If we wish to understand a phenomenon accurately, we thus cannot merely seek to elucidate our current intuitive conception of it; we must examine the phenomenon itself. And this applies as much to understanding the nature of knowledge as it does to understanding the nature of gold.

One might seek a middle ground here. Alvin Goldman has suggested that there is room both for conceptual analysis of our folk epistemological concepts as well as a more scientific epistemology that would develop epistemological concepts that depart in important ways from our folk notions. But why, on this view, do the folk notions take on any epistemological import at all, especially in light of the fact that they are bound to build in, as Goldman himself points out, false presuppositions? On Goldman's view, there must be substantial continuity between the folk notions and the more scientific ones if there is to be such a thing as epistemology at all. Without such continuity, Goldman argues, we are just changing the subject. Now I have already argued that this account of what is involved in changing the subject, an account that Goldman shares with Jackson, is not correct. Continuity of concept is merely one way to mark commonality of subject matter; causal theorists of reference have another (and to my mind, better) account. Goldman does not consider the possibility of such an account in the case of knowledge, since he regards it as simply obvious that knowledge is not a natural kind. 'Whatever one thinks about justice or consciousness as possible natural kinds, it is dubious that knowledge or justificational status are natural kinds.'[19] It is the burden of Ch. 2 to show that such a possibility cannot be so easily dismissed.

---

[19] Goldman, 'Psychology and Philosophical Analysis', in *Liaisons: Philosophy Meets the Cognitive and Social Sciences* (MIT Press, 1992), 144.

Although I do not agree with Goldman that there must inevitably be the degree of continuity he requires between our folk concepts and those of a properly scientific epistemology, I do not wish to exaggerate my disagreement with him either. After all, the account of knowledge I endorse is, in the end, a reliability account very similar to the one Goldman himself offers. Even if, however, we should discover that there is a tremendous amount of continuity between our folk epistemological notions and those of a proper scientific epistemology, it remains to be shown why our folk epistemological notions are of *epistemological* interest in their own right. Why should our folk epistemological notions be of any more interest to epistemologists than our folk chemical notions are to chemists?

Goldman responds to this challenge: 'even if one rejects the plea for continuity, a description of our epistemic folkways is in order. How would one know what to criticize, or what needs to be transcended, in the absence of such a description? So a first mission of epistemology is to describe our folkways.'[20] But if knowledge truly is a natural kind, then this sort of response is inadequate. We would hardly think that the chemist's first job is an elucidation of folk chemical notions (especially if this required extraordinary effort by the entire community of chemists over a period of millennia) so that we would know what chemical views need to be transcended. In the case of chemistry, we can simply skip straight to the project of understanding the real chemical kinds as they exist in nature. My suggestion here is that we should take seriously the possibility that a similar strategy might be equally fruitful in epistemology.

I do not mean to suggest that on the naturalistic view we will ever be able wholly to avoid appealing to our intuitions. I do think that appeals to intuition will continue to play a role in the development of philosophical views, even as theory progresses. I noted earlier that the actual practice of naturalistically minded philosophers has changed with the progress of theory so that now there is a good deal

[20] Goldman, 'Epistemic Folkways and Scientific Epistemology', ibid. 156.

more empirical examination of various phenomena rather than an exclusive reliance on appeals to intuition. But this does not mean that appeals to intuition simply drop out of the picture. Thus, for example, in philosophy of mind not so many years ago there was a good deal of discussion about whether creatures who failed to exhibit certain sorts of characteristic behavior might nevertheless be in pain. These discussions did not involve much of a look at the empirical literature on pain; instead, they relied exclusively on appeals to intuition.[21] Now, although work in philosophy of mind involves a great deal of examination of the empirical literature, we still see appeals to intuition playing a role, although the intuitions are about more esoteric matters. For example, there is discussion of what magnetosomes represent, whether it be the presence of certain sorts of magnetic fields or, instead, the presence of anaerobic conditions.

The intuitions that naturalists currently appeal to, intuitions about matters far more esoteric than what is known about Brown in Barcelona, present clear cases of theory-mediated judgment, judgment which is rightly influenced by a large body of background belief. At the same time, these judgments are phenomenologically basic; their inferential heritage is not introspectively available. More than this, these judgments are typically far less well integrated with our best available theories, and thus not nearly so well justified,[22] as our more explicitly theory-guided judgments. As the scope of our theories expands, the use of such weakly founded judgments is a necessary stepping-stone to better theory. The use of intuitive judgment does not disappear at any stage of theorizing. Instead, old intuitions give way to well-integrated theoretical judgments, and, in addition, to new intuitions about matters not yet fully captured in explicit theory.

[21] For a valuable discussion of the state of the art on this issue, see Colin Allen, 'Animal Pain', manuscript.

[22] I do not mean to be diverging here from a reliabilist account of justification. Rather, I mean only to be pointing out that allowing one's judgments to be influenced by accurate theory tends to be a source of increased reliability.

We may thus respond to the first of Bealer's objections to naturalism by pointing out that appeals to intuition do not require some non-natural faculty or a priori judgment of any sort. Bealer's argument gets off on the wrong foot by assuming that intuitions are a priori; more than this, Bealer says, the distinction between common-sense empirical judgment and intuition is 'obvious' (p. 165). Obvious it may be to those opposed to naturalism, but the appeal to a priority is, of course, contentious in this context. Bealer is right to think that naturalists owe us an explanation of their practice of appealing to intuition, especially in light of their rejection of the a priori. At the same time, I hope I have shown that this explanation is one that naturalists may easily provide. The practice of appealing to intuition has no non-natural ingredients.

1.4 Naturalism and rules of inference

Bealer argues that naturalists are not only unable to account for their own philosophical practice, but that naturalistic scruples leave little room for legitimate belief about any subject, since 'following rules and procedures—for example, rules of inference' (p. 167) requires an acknowledgement of the force of a priori intuition. And Laurence BonJour comments, 'the practice of even those who most explicitly reject the idea of substantive *a priori* justification inevitably involves tacit appeal to insights and modes of reasoning that can only be understood as *a priori* in character, if they are justified at all.'[23] As BonJour points out, this leaves naturalists in an unenviable position: 'we see that the repudiation of all *a priori* justification is apparently tantamount to the repudiation of argument or reasoning generally, thus amounting in effect to intellectual suicide.'[24] But naturalists do not see the following of rules and procedures, in particular, the role of rules of inference, in the way in which Bealer and BonJour do.

***

[23] BonJour, *In Defense of Pure Reason*, p. ix.   [24] Ibid. 5.

Naturalists, of course, make inferences, and they need to account for the legitimacy of this practice, at least in those cases in which it is legitimate. The legitimacy of an inference, on the naturalist view, is dependent upon its reliability: reliable inferential practices are epistemically legitimate; those which are unreliable are not. We must thus engage in a project of self-examination, in which we scrutinize our own epistemic practice. We wish to examine the inferential rules that underlie our practice of belief acquisition, and to the extent that we find unreliable inference patterns at work, we need to re-examine and modify our own practice. The empirical work involved in understanding our inferential habits is well underway, as is the assessment of its epistemological importance.

Reliability is the naturalist's standard here.[25] Meeting a priori standards is simply irrelevant. Rules of inference that tend to produce true beliefs in the kinds of environments that human beings occupy may fail to live up to a priori standards of cogency, but they are none the worse for that. By the same token, rules of inference that do meet a priori standards may be unworkable in practice or hopelessly mired in problems of computational complexity. These kinds of problems are not in any way ameliorated if the rules do meet a priori standards of cogency. A priori standards thus drop out of the picture entirely as simply irrelevant to proper epistemic practice. They fail to bear on the conduct of enquiry.[26]

A naturalistic account of proper belief acquisition thus does not need to appeal to a priori intuition of appropriate principles of inference. Recognition of appropriate inferential patterns is an empirical affair for the naturalist. More than this, justified belief, on at least one widely held naturalistic account, is a matter of reliable belief production and does not itself require recognition of that reliability.

---

[25] Why this should be so will be discussed in Ch. 2.

[26] It is thus particularly ironic that Mark Kaplan both criticizes naturalistic epistemology as irrelevant to the conduct of enquiry and simultaneously defends the importance of a priori standards of cogent argument. See Kaplan, 'Epistemology Denatured', 350–65.

Naturalistic scruples about appropriate belief production thus leave room for a great deal of knowledge.

1.5 Naturalism and epistemic terminology

Let me turn then to the last of Bealer's charges against naturalism, that in eschewing a priori intuition, naturalism leaves no room for epistemic terminology. This charge too, I believe, falls short of its mark. While the account naturalists give of epistemic terminology is anything but uncontroversial, it should not be controversial that naturalists have an account of that terminology that satisfies their own epistemic standards. The suggestion that naturalism is self-defeating is thus turned aside.

Epistemology, according to naturalism, investigates a certain natural phenomenon, namely, knowledge, and the term 'knowledge' and other epistemic idioms gain their reference in much the same way that natural-kind terms do. Now supposing that terms like 'knowledge' gain their reference in this way is not without its presuppositions, as I pointed out earlier. The phenomenon we call knowledge must have a certain degree of theoretical unity if reference is to be secured. Were we to discover that there is no more theoretical unity to the various items we call knowledge than there is to the set consisting of ships and shoes and sealing wax, then a presupposition of the introduction of the term would be undermined, and the view that there is no such thing as knowledge would be sustained. But naturalists, and indeed, most non-naturalists, do not think that such a possibility is at all likely.[27] Indeed, almost all epistemologists believe that there is a great deal of unity to the phenomenon of human knowledge. If there is indeed such a unity, one goal of epistemology is to say what it consists in. And of course if it should

[27] But see Michael Williams, *Unnatural Doubts: Epistemological Realism and the Basis of Skepticism* (Princeton University Press, 1996).

turn out there is no such unity, then one goal of epistemology would be to make that fact plain.

The investigation of the phenomenon of knowledge, on the naturalist's view, is an empirical investigation, and the legitimacy of epistemic terminology depends on its properly latching on to genuine, theoretically unified kinds. That is all that naturalistic scruples require. Because epistemology thus conceived is a wholly empirical investigation, naturalists have nothing here to apologize for. Their terminology earns its keep in just the way that chemical or biological or physical terminology earns its keep: it must be part of a successful empirical theory. The fact that terms such as 'knowledge' are not part of physics or chemistry does not show that they are not naturalistically acceptable. Rather, the question for naturalists is whether knowledge turns out to be a theoretically unified phenomenon, and this gives every appearance of being a legitimate and tractable empirical question.

Some will say that this enterprise, because it is descriptive, fails to engage the normative dimension of epistemological theorizing. They will argue that it is only by removing knowledge from the empirical realm, and making it the object of a priori investigation, that its normative character may emerge. This is an issue I want to discuss in detail later (in Ch. 5), but for now it is possible to say something brief that will go some distance toward responding to this challenge. The empirical investigation of knowledge may well reveal a phenomenon worthy of our pursuit. Surely such a suggestion does not require a degree of optimism ungrounded in fact. But this is all the normativity that our epistemic notions require. We should not suppose that the investigation of knowledge must be non-empirical if we are to be able to explain why knowledge is worth having.[28]

---

[28] Nor is it clear why a non-empirical investigation, if such were possible, would go any distance at all toward addressing the normativity issue. Much of the criticism of naturalism on this score has been, I believe, entirely beside the point. While it is correctly pointed out that it is hard to see how an empirical investigation could address

Epistemic terminology, and, indeed, philosophical terminology in general, must be grounded in the world if it is to be naturalistically legitimate. This does not require that such terminology appear in our physical theories, for naturalists need not accept any sort of reductionism. Once we regard epistemology as the investigation of a certain natural phenomenon, we clear the way for distinctively epistemic terminology. Naturalism would only threaten to eliminate epistemic terminology as illegitimate if there were no prospect of discovering theoretically unified epistemic phenomena. But there is little reason, I believe, to think that this is currently a genuine possibility. Moreover, if there were reason to worry on this account, it would spell the demise not only of naturalistic epistemology, but epistemology generally. Bealer's final objection, that naturalists are not entitled to the very epistemic terminology they make use of, thus ultimately fails.

1.6 The autonomy of philosophy

I want to close this chapter by addressing one further issue, a concern that, I believe, motivates Bealer's attack on naturalism, and this has to do with the autonomy of philosophy. In a lengthy attack[29] on the kind of scientific essentialism I favor, Bealer begins by suggesting that naturalism raises the possibility that science will somehow 'eclipse' philosophy. Naturalism threatens the autonomy of philosophical enquiry, Bealer argues, and it is thus only by rejecting naturalism that we may make room for a distinctively philosophical enterprise.[30] BonJour has a similar conception of philosophical

our normative concerns, critics of naturalism take this to count in favor of some sort of a priori investigation. But neither is it clear how an a priori investigation could address those concerns. The appropriate conclusion, I believe, is that we simply don't currently see how normative concerns can be addressed at all. This does not count for or against any particular view.

[29] Bealer, 'The Philosophical Limits of Scientific Essentialism'.
[30] For a related concern, see the objection due to Fumerton discussed in sect. 6.2 below.

endeavors: 'philosophy is *a priori* if it is anything (or at least if it is anything intellectually respectable)'.[31] But then the naturalistic rejection of the a priori results immediately in a repudiation of philosophy itself. As Bealer and BonJour see it, if naturalism is right, we should all give up doing philosophy and take up science instead.

Now I myself have a high regard for philosophy. Although I am a naturalist, I do not believe that philosophy must be eliminated. Naturalists do not regard philosophy as illegitimate, nor do they see it as in any way threatened by the progress of science. At the same time, we do not wish to grant philosophy the degree of autonomy that Bealer, BonJour, and other opponents of naturalism would favor. There are important issues here, and it is worth making clear just where naturalism stands on them.

Questions about knowledge and justification, questions about theory and evidence, are, to my mind, legitimate questions, and they are ones in which philosophy has a special stake. The questions that philosophers wish to ask about these topics are different from those addressed by historians, sociologists, and psychologists, but no less important or intellectually respectable. If the autonomy of a discipline consists in its dealing with a distinctive set of questions, or in approaching certain phenomena with a distinctive set of concerns, then philosophy is surely an autonomous discipline. There is no danger that these questions and concerns will somehow be co-opted by other disciplines.

When Bealer raises the issue of philosophy's autonomy, however, he has in mind something quite different from this. For Bealer, the autonomy of philosophy is identified with the claim that philosophical knowledge is a priori, entirely independent of anything the empirical sciences have to offer. Now this, of course, is a claim any naturalist will want to reject. On the naturalist's view, philosophical questions are continuous with the empirical sciences. Work in the empirical sciences is deeply relevant to philosophical questions, and

---

[31] BonJour, *In Defense of Pure Reason*, p. ix.

our philosophical theories are constrained and guided by results in other disciplines. It is worth noting that the special sciences are not autonomous in anything like Bealer's sense, i.e. they are not wholly independent of work in other disciplines. Work in biology is not wholly independent of chemistry; sociology is not wholly independent of psychology; and so on. But the loss of this sort of autonomy does not rob these disciplines of their legitimacy, nor does it threaten the special sciences with the loss of their distinctive subject matter. Biologists need not fear that their field will be taken away from them by chemists once it is recognized that chemistry is relevant to biological concerns.

So too with philosophy. In recognizing that philosophy is continuous with the sciences, we need not fear that philosophy will thereby be 'eclipsed' by science. The constraints that science presents for philosophical theorizing should be welcomed, for philosophical theorizing unconstrained by empirical fact loses its connection with the very phenomena which we, as philosophers, seek to understand. Philosophy is an autonomous discipline, in the sense that it addresses a distinctive set of questions and concerns, and in this respect it is no more nor less autonomous than physics or chemistry or biology. This is surely all the autonomy we should want. It is, in any case, all the autonomy that we may have.

1.7 Conclusion

Bealer's multi-count indictment of naturalism is not supported by the facts. We can make perfectly good sense of a thoroughly empirical philosophy, one that does not assign either the weight or the provenance to intuition that Bealer and others do. Epistemology is fully naturalized when it regards knowledge as a natural phenomenon, an object of study with a substantial degree of theoretical unity to it. And with the burden of this indictment now discharged, we may turn to an investigation of knowledge itself.

2

Knowledge as Natural Phenomenon

WHERE should we turn, and how should we proceed, if we are to investigate the phenomenon of knowledge itself? It is not necessary to found a new discipline here, for there is already a good deal of empirical work on the subject. One of the more fruitful areas of such research is cognitive ethology[1]. There is a large literature on animal[2] cognition, and workers in this field typically speak of animals knowing a great many things. They see animal knowledge as a legitimate object of study, a phenomenon with a good deal of theoretical integrity to it. Knowledge, as it is portrayed in this literature, does

---

[1] My use of the term 'cognitive ethology' requires some comment. The term was introduced by Donald Griffin (see his books *The Question of Animal Awareness*, 2nd edn. (Rockefeller University Press, 1981); *Animal Thinking* (Harvard University Press, 1984); and *Animal Minds* (University of Chicago Press, 1992)) to denote the study of animal consciousness. In spite of Griffin's formative usage, it is quite natural to use the term for the study of animal cognition generally, as Alan Kamil notes ('On the Proper Definition of Cognitive Ethology', in R. Balda, I. M. Pepperberg, and A. C. Kamil (eds.), *Animal Cognition in Nature: The Convergence of Psychology and Biology in Laboratory and Field* (Academic Press, 1998), 22), as many already do, and that is the way I will use it here.

[2] I will speak indifferently here of 'animal' cognition. There are, of course, substantial cognitive differences among animals. The notion of knowledge one finds in this body of literature, however, abstracts away from those very substantial differences.

causal and explanatory work. The goal of this chapter is to make clear just what this phenomenon is that cognitive ethologists are studying, and to make clear just why it is that they see this as a phenomenon with such a large degree of theoretical integrity. If cognitive ethologists are even roughly right, then talk of animal knowledge is not a mere *façon de parler*; rather, there really is such a thing as animal knowledge. Knowledge constitutes a legitimate scientific category. In a word, it is a natural kind.

Now some will be happy to acknowledge this much, at least for the sake of argument, but still wish to deny that we are yet talking about a proper object of philosophical investigation. Humans are, after all, smarter than the average bear, and this added intelligence makes human knowledge a different thing altogether from the kind of knowledge studied by cognitive ethologists. More than this, it is the features distinctive of human knowledge that make it philosophically interesting. Cognitive ethologists may talk about knowledge in any way they please, on this way of viewing things; but it has nothing to do with the philosophically interesting kind of knowledge.

There are a number of different sources of this sort of challenge to the project I am engaged in here. We will need to look at them in detail. Whatever the sources of the challenge may be, it is clearly true that in order for my project to go through, we need to show not only that there is a legitimate scientific category of animal knowledge, but also that this scientific category is of philosophical interest.

Fair enough. But we need to take things one at a time. This chapter has a modest goal. It is not addressed to the question of whether animal knowledge is a philosophically interesting category or whether human knowledge is different in kind from the knowledge of other animals. Instead, this chapter deals with the phenomenon of animal knowledge as it arises in the literature of cognitive ethology. I will, in later chapters, argue that this is indeed a philosophically interesting sort of knowledge, and I will also argue that human knowledge is not different in kind from the knowledge to be found in the rest of the animal world. Indeed, I will argue that the kind of knowledge that philosophers have talked about all along just is the kind of knowledge that cognitive ethologists are currently studying. But here, in this chapter, our concerns are more mundane: What is animal knowledge? Why do cognitive ethologists study it? What kind of causal and explanatory role does talk of knowledge play in the theories under review?

2.1 Intentional idioms in the literature on animal behavior

Cognitive ethologists use a rich vocabulary of intentional idioms in describing animal behavior. One standard textbook, John Alcock's *Animal Behavior*,[3] has section headings referring to 'hiding from', 'spotting', 'evading', and 'repelling' predators. Wolves are described as chasing a herd of caribou or a number of solitary moose 'before finally selecting a vulnerable individual to attack in earnest'.[4] Hunting dogs are described as having an 'intended victim'.[5] Rats, Alcock comments, 'avidly explore areas around their burrows to learn the salient features of their habitat, information that will be of more than passing interest to them if pursued by a predator'.[6]

Another text, Jacques Vauclair's *Animal Cognition*[7], discusses spatial representation in animals in the following terms:

Most animal species move about in their environment, searching for food and for partners, escaping predators, or finding resting places. These kinds of movement presuppose at least a fixed reference location (e.g., 'home') to which the animal must return. Except in those situations in which a landmark is constantly present either at the start of a journey or at its end, the animal is continually faced with changing information influencing its knowledge of its position and the position of objects in the environment.

---

[3] John Alcock, *Animal Behavior: An Evolutionary Approach* (Sinauer, 1975).

[4] Ibid. 353.   [5] Ibid.   [6] Ibid. 216–17.

[7] Jacques Vauclair, *Animal Cognition: An Introduction to Modern Comparative Psychology* (Harvard University Press, 1996), 62.

And Bernd Heinrich[8] discusses co-operative hunting in ravens in this way:

George Schaller told me of watching raven pairs in Mongolia cooperate in snatching rats from feeding raptors. Similarly, in Yellowstone Park, Ray Paunovich reported seeing a red-tailed hawk with a ground squirrel. Two ravens approached. One distracted the hawk from the front while the other handily snatched the squirrel from behind. Carsten Hinnerichs saw the same maneuver repeated three times in a row in a field near Brücke, Germany, where a fox was catching field mice. Terry McEneaney, Yellowstone Park ornithologist, observed two ravens circling an osprey nest where the female osprey was incubating. One raven landed on the nest rim and took a fish, then while the osprey was distracted by this thief, the other raven swooped down and stole an osprey egg.

These examples are not the exception in the animal behavior literature; they are the rule. Animal behavior is consistently described in intentional terms, and intentional idioms are not reserved for primates or the family pet. As Carolyn Ristau comments, in her work on piping plovers,

I particularly chose to study birds not because a purposive interpretation of their behavior is clear-cut or because we are easily able to empathize with their possible communications and mental states (as we seem to with apes and our pet dogs), but because it is difficult to do either. These very obstacles may help us to specify the evidence for such an interpretation more carefully and to suggest possible levels in the transition from rudimentary to more full-fledged knowledge and purposes . . .[9]

The investigators who routinely make use of intentional terminology in their descriptions of animal behavior are not wooly-minded pet owners[10] eager to attribute the most sophisticated cognitive

---

[8] Bernd Heinrich, *Mind of the Raven: Investigations and Adventures with Wolf-Birds* (Harper Collins, 1999), 133.

[9] Carolyn Ristau, 'Aspects of the Cognitive Ethology of an Injury-Feigning Bird, the Piping Plover', in Ristau (ed.), *Cognitive Ethology: The Minds of Other Animals* (Lawrence Erlbaum, 1991), 93.

[10] The term 'wooly-minded' is not meant to be redundant here; it describes a certain sort of pet owner.

attributes on the basis of the slightest tweak of paw, hoof, or beak. Intentional vocabulary in the description of animal behavior is, instead, a standard feature of the serious scientific literature.

I do not mean to suggest that the mere fact that these intentional idioms are used in a serious body of scientific literature should be taken to settle definitively the question of whether such usage is legitimate. Indeed, I will turn immediately to the question of the legitimacy of this usage. At the same time, I do believe that the fact that this usage is now well entrenched in the scientific literature is strong prima-facie evidence of its legitimacy, and that those who are skeptical of the legitimacy of such usage should see the entrenchment of this vocabulary as a strong prima-facie difficulty for their position. A priori arguments against well-established scientific research programs have a history of failure. Allegedly extra-scientific insights into the limits of science have not fared well. If we wish to know whether non-human animals have intentional states, we would thus do well to look at the empirical literature on non-human animals in order to see what work the talk of intentional states performs within these theories. As with any other existence claim in science—that there are electrons; that there are genes; that there are tectonic plates—the claim that there are intentional states in non-human animals is shown to be worthy of belief by way of its role in a successful theory. Let us see what that role is.

2.2 Animal behavior

A natural thought here is that we should begin by looking at the data on animal behavior, where by 'data' we mean descriptions of animal behavior in non-intentional terms. Just what kinds of bodily motions do various non-human animals engage in, and what is it about this behavior that calls for an explanation in terms of intentional states? Natural as this thought is, however, the attempt to approach the animal behavior literature in this way is frequently frustrated because the description of animal behavior itself is so often given in intentional terms.

Consider Bernd Heinrich's remarks about ravens, quoted above. Heinrich speaks of ravens 'distracting' hawks and osprey. He comments that an observer in Germany saw a particular bit of raven behavior repeated three times, and that similar behavior was observed in a variety of other locations. But how should we characterize the behavior that was repeatedly observed? It is not described in terms of bodily motions. Heinrich does not speak of the ravens moving their beaks, or wings or bodies in certain patterns. Indeed, there is no reason to think that the manner in which the ravens distracted their various targets involved any commonality at all at the level of bodily motion. There are bits of animal behavior that may be described in such terms, but this does not seem to be such a case. Instead, what is common to the various episodes described can only be appreciated by attributing certain intentional states to the animals involved. If we see the behavior as a case of one bird distracting another, we are able to make sense of it in a way that a description in terms of moving beaks, wings, and bodies fails to capture.

When one human being tries to distract another, the various bits of bodily motion need have nothing in common with one another when described in non-intentional terms. Someone who insisted on finding some commonality at that level of description before using a single term to characterize the various behaviors would for that very reason fail to see cases of distraction as tokens of a single type. The same is true of animal behavior. When ravens attempt to distract other birds, they no more engage in a common form of bodily motion than do human beings trying to distract one another.

This does not mean, of course, that observers cannot describe the various behaviors in non-intentional terms. There are descriptions of wing-flapping, squawking, pecking, and so on. When described in non-intentional terms, however, these behaviors are entirely heterogeneous. It is only when construed intentionally that the otherwise heterogeneous bits of behavior may be seen as instances of a single kind. Our recognition that ravens work co-operatively with one another to distract other birds and steal their food allows us to explain and predict subsequent behavior, thereby providing us with explanations and predictions that we would not have were we to limit our descriptions of the behaviors to non-intentional terms. The non-intentional descriptions fail to capture what it is that the various behaviors have in common. We lose our ability to recognize subsequent repetitions of the same behavior if we insist on characterizing it as bits of bodily motion.

Indeed, notice that it is impossible in practice to describe animal behavior in any meaningful way without introducing descriptions of that behavior that go far beyond talk of motions of body parts. Consider the classical categories of feeding, fighting, flight, and sexual reproduction. It is safe to say that no work on animal behavior can fail to take these categories seriously as legitimate objects of study, areas with a certain theoretical integrity to them. But none of these categories can be defined in terms of mere motions of body parts. Consider flight, for example. Animals move their legs rapidly, or their wings, for a variety of reasons. The difference between behavior that is rightly described as flight, and mere running, or playing, must make reference, however implicitly, to the reasons for the behavior. But once we talk about reasons we have moved squarely within the intentional realm. The characterization of animal behavior itself, and not merely its explanation, requires intentional terminology.

Consider locomotion. Animals move around in their environment, and the manner in which they move is anything but random. Birds build nests which they leave for feeding but to which they later return; bees leave the hive only to return; beavers leave their lodges and later return. In each of these cases, the animal in question has a certain ability, and we may investigate just how it is that the animal is able to negotiate its environment. Put a different way, the environment makes certain informational demands on the animal. What we wish to know is how it is that the animal is able to respond to those informational demands.

Now one of the simplest ways for an animal to negotiate its return to a particular location is by the technique of dead reckoning. Desert ants (*Cataglyphis fortis*), for example, leave their nests to search for food, but return directly to their nest as soon as prey is captured.[11] While the path from nest to prey may be highly indirect, the path from prey back to the nest is not. How is it that the ant is able to return to its home, and by such a direct route, after its search for food? One clue to the technique used is found when the investigator picks up the ant after it captures its prey, putting it down in a different location. The ant does not, in this case, return to its nest. Instead, it travels along a path parallel to the one it would have taken were it left undisturbed. Thus, if a path 50 meters long and due west would have taken the ant back to its nest had it been left alone, the ant will take a path 50 meters long and due west even after it has been picked up and moved. At this point, the ant begins to circle in a fruitless attempt to find its nest.

While this technique is highly effective in allowing ants to return to their nests in their natural environment, that is, in the absence of meddlesome investigators, it is one of the cruder methods of finding one's way home. It is, for example, completely insensitive to any of the landmarks on the return trip. At the same time, dead reckoning does require some highly non-trivial skills: the ant must, on its trip from nest to prey, be able to keep a running tab on its distance and direction from the nest. Since the location of the prey is not known to the ant at the start of the trip, the outward path is highly irregular. Keeping track of the distance and direction from the nest is thus itself an important cognitive achievement.

The technique of dead reckoning is found in a wide range of animals. Aside from ants, it is present in bees, wasps, spiders, hamsters,

[11] See e.g. Sara Shettleworth, *Cognition, Evolution, and Behavior* (Oxford, 1998), 281–3.

gerbils, and geese, as well as many other animals.[12] The crudeness of the technique also explains its usefulness. The fact that dead reckoning is insensitive even to large changes in features of the landscape makes it appear quite crude, not only in the presence of an investigator willing to move the subject animal over large distances, but also in the presence of a mild wind blowing the animal off course. But another way to put this point illustrates its strength: the animal requires a minimum of information about features of its environment in order to orient itself by dead reckoning, and this allows the technique to be used, for example, in the dark, when visual information is hard to come by, or in desert environments which are largely devoid of usable landmarks.

There are a very large number of other techniques for achieving some understanding of spatial location, techniques that may be used instead of or in conjunction with dead reckoning. For example, some animals make use of beacons, i.e. cues such as odors or sounds emanating from their goal; landmarks; geometrical features of the environment; or the direction and angle of the sun or stars.[13] In each case, the circumstances and manner in which such information is made use of is subject to experimental investigation. But the only way in which one can make sense of an animal's ability to move around in its environment is by viewing it as engaged in certain information-processing tasks. The animal is approaching its environment with certain cognitive abilities, and these abilities allow it to extract information from its encounters with that environment.

Animal behavior thus cannot adequately be described, let alone explained, if we insist on narrowly circumscribing our vocabulary to talk of the motions of bodily parts. Even some of the fairly crude behavior of ants requires that we allow for internal states with informational content. Informational content by itself, however, falls short of true mental representation. Thermostats have internal

[12] See e.g. Sara Shettleworth, *Cognition, Evolution, and Behavior* (Oxford, 1998), 282–3. [13] Ibid. 279–332.

states that register information about their environment; they do not, however, have mental states. And even allowing for the existence of mental states with informational content does not, by itself, give us belief. In the human case, for example, there are subdoxastic states that are bearers of information; no adequate account of human perception, for example, or language acquisition, can fail to allow for such states. So even though we must allow that animals have internal states that are bearers of information, still more needs to be said in order to make out the case for animal belief.

2.3 From information-bearing states to belief

Animals have certain needs and our understanding of their behavior is informed by our recognition of these needs. Animals need to eat. They need to avoid predators. They need to reproduce. Our ability to recognize behavior as feeding behavior, or predator avoidance behavior, or reproductive behavior presupposes at least a minimal understanding of these needs. A more refined understanding is achieved when we recognize how it is that features of the animals' environment bear on these biologically given needs. And an adequate understanding of the relationship between environment and animal cognition must be constrained and informed by a recognition of the fact that animals are a product of evolution.

The environment places certain informational demands on an animal. If it is to satisfy its biologically given needs, it will need to recognize certain features of its environment and the evolutionary process must thereby assure that an animal has the cognitive capacities that allow it to deal effectively with that environment. What this requires is the ability to represent information. The ant that proceeds by dead reckoning from its food back to its nest must, all along the way, represent its distance and direction from the nest. Ravens co-operating in attempting to steal a dead squirrel from a hawk must keep track of what the hawk is attending to if the attempt is to have any chance of success. This requires a subtle monitoring process that can only be described in informational terms. Precisely which features of the environment are being represented in any particular case of animal behavior will involve subtle questions that can only be resolved through extensive investigation, but it is beyond dispute that the animal will need to represent features of its environment if it is to deal with it effectively at all.

Once we recognize the existence of internally represented animal needs together with representations of features of the environment, we have the beginnings of a belief–desire psychology. The ravens distract the hawk because they are hungry; they want to steal the hawk's egg; they believe that by attempting to take the squirrel away from the hawk, they will thereby be able to take the egg. Just as we explain human action by attributing beliefs and desires as causes of action, we explain the behavior of a wide variety of animals as the causal consequence of their beliefs and desires. The attribution of beliefs and desires to non-human animals is neither less explanatory nor less well motivated than it is in the case of humans. In both cases, the attribution of beliefs and desires demonstrates its legitimacy by way of its role in a theory that provides successful prediction and explanation.

Now it is certainly true that there are some organisms[14] that have needs and that are responsive to features of their environment and yet, all the same, should not be credited with a belief–desire psychology. Consider plants. They need sunlight in order to survive and they turn toward the sun in order better to make sunlight available for photosynthesis. We do not, in this case, credit the plant with a desire for sunlight and a belief that sunlight is to be found in a certain location. What is the difference between the 'behavior' of the plant and the behavior of the ravens? Why is it that we need to attribute beliefs and desires to the ravens in order to explain their behavior, and yet do not need to attribute beliefs and desires to plants in order to explain theirs?

[14] And some non-organisms.

One is tempted to say here that in the case of the plant, but not the raven, there is a lower-level explanation for the motion of the plant toward the sun, and in so far as there is such an explanation, the psychological explanation is thereby undermined. I think that this is in fact correct, but one needs to tread carefully here. One might have the idea that the motion of plants can be explained in physical terms, thereby obviating the need for a mentalistic explanation, but one does not want to suggest that animals are not entirely physically composed or that there is no sort of physical story to be told about the causal antecedents of animal behavior. And similarly, those who are skeptical about the attribution of mental states to animals had better not suggest that the reason for their doubt is that animal behavior must ultimately be in some sense physical, for if this is a reason to worry about the attribution of mental states to animals, it is equally a reason to worry about the attribution of mental states to humans. The reason for rejecting the psychological explanation of plant motion is not that plants are physically composed. It is instead that plant behavior can be explained in lower-level terms. Such lower-level explanation requires more than mere physical composition.

To take an example from Jerry Fodor, camshafts are, from the point of view of physics, a heterogeneous lot; they do not form a natural kind in physics. Camshafts come in different sizes, different shapes, different weights; they are made of a variety of different materials. Nevertheless, we are all camshaft materialists; we all recognize that camshafts are entirely composed of physical stuff. We speak of camshafts, and regard them as a kind in explaining the behavior of automobiles, because there are properties that all camshafts share and which serve to explain a range of automobile behavior. Someone who did not recognize the existence of camshafts as a kind would fail to see important commonalities among different cars and thereby regard as entirely heterogeneous various phenomena which may be brought under the umbrella of a single explanation. When several different cars each fail to run because their camshafts are all broken, there is a common problem that they share even if their camshafts are, from the physicist's point of view, quite different. An automobile mechanic who failed to recognize the commonality here would be missing something important about these vehicles.

Although the behavior of each individual camshaft is the product of physical forces generated by the physical properties of the material of which it is composed, there is not some single physical explanation for the failure of all the camshafts; from a physical perspective, their shortcomings may be quite heterogeneous. Adverting to the higher-level property and thereby abstracting from the physical details of the camshafts' composition allows us to capture these commonalities. If there are important generalizations to be captured at this level, then the study of auto mechanics will gain some legitimacy.

As Fodor has argued, what is true of auto mechanics is true of psychology, and indeed, of the special sciences generally.[15] While human beings are entirely physically composed, this does not entail that the physical states on which mental state types supervene form a kind in physics. Just as camshafts may be heterogeneous from the point of view of physics, the class of beliefs that two and two is four may be heterogeneous from the point of view of physics. And if it is, one should not thereby conclude that it doesn't form a legitimate kind in psychology. The legitimacy of talk about beliefs, where beliefs are identified by their content, is secured by showing that this allows for a psychological theory that succeeds in prediction and explanation. No doubt beliefs are entirely physically composed; but this does not require that they form a homogeneous physical kind.

Now the reason for appealing to mental representations such as beliefs in the case of animals is much the same as the reason for

---

[15] In many places, but perhaps best in 'Special Sciences', in *Representations: Philosophical Essays on the Foundations of Cognitive Science* (MIT Press, 1981).

talking about properties of camshafts in the case of automobiles. There are commonalities among animals that can be captured at the level of talk of belief but cannot be captured in any lower-level vocabulary. A raven, for example, comes to believe that a hawk has been distracted, and thus attempts to steal its egg. Other ravens, similarly placed, behave in a similar way, and for much the same reason. But there is no reason to think that the various ravens, each of which form a belief about some target hawk, have a common physical state in their brains. There is, in particular, no more reason to think this about the ravens than there is to think this about human beings all of whom share a common belief. So we need to advert to some common property of the various individuals that abstracts from the details of the physical level of description.

The need to appeal to some higher-level property, however, does not, by itself, make the case for talk of mental representations or beliefs. Even if the mechanisms of phototropy were chemically heterogeneous, this would not, by itself, make a case for mental representations in plants. Mental representations are a particular sort of higher-level property. They are states whose interactions with one another need to be explained in informational terms. When we talk about beliefs, for example, they are individuated by their informational content. Propositional attitudes in general are so-called precisely because it is their propositional, or informational, content by which they are typed. So when we look at a bit of animal behavior, one question we need to ask is whether its explanation requires talk of informational content, or whether some lower-level explanation, whether chemical or otherwise, will do.

Notice that when a plant responds to the presence of sunlight by moving toward it, if information about the presence of sunlight is registered in the plant, the sole role that that information plays is in getting the plant to move in the direction of the light; the information about the sunlight is not available for other, more diverse, informational interactions. When you and I come to believe that sunlight is present in a particular direction, however, that information is available to interact with our other internal states so as to inform an extremely wide range of behavior. It is this fact about us that requires talk not merely of a representational system of information-bearing states, but talk of beliefs. The motion of plants toward the sun requires no such thing. Plant motion is directly responsive to certain stimuli. Famously, human behavior typically is not. When the sun shines on us, we may move toward it if we are in the mood for a suntan or warmth, or away from it if we are worried about skin cancer. Merely knowing that we've registered the presence of sunlight does nothing for predicting human behavior; it is all that is required for predicting the motion of plants. Predicting human behavior thus requires reference to both beliefs and desires. Predicting plant motion requires neither; reference to stimulus conditions is sufficient.

The elaborate behavior of ravens in distracting a hawk so as to steal her egg is not a simple response triggered by some environmental condition. While the behavior is straightforwardly explained by appealing to beliefs and desires, no one has ever offered an explanation of such complex behaviors in terms that obviate the need for representational states. Nor is the case of stealing the egg an unusual one in the animal behavior literature. What we see is a wide range of animal behavior,[16] in a wide range of different species, that has straightforward explanations in terms of beliefs and desires, and no competing alternative explanations. In circumstances such as these, a reluctance to endorse the available explanatory scheme does not seem cautious; rather, it seems unmotivated.

[16]   Where to draw the line between those animals whose behavior can be explained in terms of sub-doxastic information-bearing states and those whose behavior can only be explained by a belief–desire psychology is a difficult empirical question. Drawing this line, however, is not necessary for the project of this book as long as it is clear, as I have argued, that the line does not place humans on one side and all other animals on the other. (For discussion of the irrelevance of language use to this issue, see below, sect. 3.2.) I am very much indebted in this section to Colin Allen and Marc Bekoff, *Species of Mind: The Philosophy and Biology of Cognitive Ethology* (MIT Press, 1997), ch. 5, as well as personal communications with Colin Allen.

2.4 Fear of anthropomorphism

The animal behavior literature was dominated for decades, just as the rest of the literature in psychology was, by behaviorism. Under the influence of behaviorist strictures, it was illegitimate to talk of intentional states not only in non-human animals, but in human beings as well. As one well-known joke had it, while other psychologists worried about anthropomorphizing animal behavior, Skinner and his followers worried about anthropomorphizing human behavior.

The literature on human psychology has largely weathered the storm of behaviorism, and talk of intentional states in humans is no longer regarded as something for which psychologists must apologize. But the animal behavior literature is quite different. Talk of intentional states in animals is still regarded with suspicion in many quarters, and it is treated with great caution by almost all. Why should this be?

It is interesting here to compare the animal behavior literature with the literature on cognition in human infants. It is now universally agreed upon by developmental psychologists that, even apart from the influence of behaviorism, the cognitive sophistication of infants was systematically underestimated for years. Even now, the full extent of the infant's cognitive sophistication is not well understood. But what calls for explanation in looking at the literature on infants in the last several decades—as I say, even apart from the influence of behaviorism—is what appears to be a deep asymmetry in the disutility that has been attached to two kinds of errors one might make in explaining infant behavior. While one wants one's explanations to be accurate, of course, one would expect in the ordinary course of events that some hypotheses offered to explain infant behavior would attribute too much intellectual sophistication to the infant, while others would attribute too little. Moreover, one would expect that, looking at a large body of literature over an extended period of time, one should see a fair bit of each sort of mistake. That is, from the perspective of our current, and presumably improved understanding of infant cognition, one should see many cases in which earlier theorists proposed explanations attributing far more cognitive sophistication to their subjects than do current theories, and one should also see about equally as many cases of the opposite sort of error. But in practice what one sees, almost exclusively, is gross underestimation, relative to current understanding, of the sophistication of infant cognition. It is as if developmental psychologists have had to be dragged, kicking and screaming, to a recognition of the cognitive abilities of infants.

Hand in hand with this reluctance to attribute sophisticated cognition to infants has been a certain attitude toward evidence of infant cognitive abilities. While laboratory experimentation has long been, to my mind, rightly recognized as an important source of information, other potential sources of information have been largely ignored. In particular, consider the experience of parents, who do, after all, spend a tremendous amount of time with their children, and would be expected, on that ground alone, to be quite knowledgeable about at least some aspects of infant behavior and cognition. The claims of parents, and especially mothers, about their children have been almost entirely ignored in the infant development literature. They are regarded as 'anecdotal', or worse. Now the idea that parents' beliefs about their own children are potentially biased is not, of course, in any way unreasonable. There is a great deal of reason to think that parents are especially prone to make certain sorts of mistakes about their own children, just as there is ample literature to support the claim that individuals are particularly prone to make certain sorts of errors in judgments about themselves. But while this gives one good reason to treat parental accounts of infant behavior with caution, and, more than that, to be especially sensitive to certain sorts of biased reporting, this kind of treatment is altogether different from the actual practice one sees in the developmental literature, a practice of simply ignoring a potentially rich body of relevant data and explanatory hypotheses. Indeed, with the benefit of hindsight, we can say that even if parental accounts were grossly to overestimate the intellectual sophistication of infants, taking them seriously would have presented a useful counter to the hypotheses and perspectives that were actually taken seriously.

In looking at the animal behavior literature over the last several decades, one sees a similar trend. First, there has been a steadily increasing recognition of the intellectual sophistication of non-human animals. To put the point another way, from the perspective of current theorizing, work on animals in the past has systematically underestimated their cognitive abilities. At the same time, the rate at which the animal behavior literature has wised up, as it were, is considerably slower than the literature on infant cognition. In addition, there is a similarity in the way in which data have been handled. Data from both pet owners and animal trainers have been largely ignored. Again, the idea that there might be certain sorts of errors to which pet owners or animal trainers are especially liable is not, by any means, foolish. But this does not justify a practice of simply ignoring such data entirely, let alone failing to consider the accounts of such individuals as a useful source of explanatory hypotheses worthy of careful testing. Moreover, the sound idea that pet owners and animal trainers might be biased in their background theories about the animal world, while correct, not only fails to distinguish them from any other potential source of information; in particular, it fails to distinguish them from professional psychologists studying animal behavior, who may be susceptible to certain biased background theories of their own. Indeed, when one looks at the trends in the animal behavior literature over the past few decades and sees the extent to which animal cognition has been systematically underrated by current lights, the suggestion that there has been such a bias on the part of psychologists studying animal behavior is at least worthy of serious consideration.

Consider Sara Shettleworth's attempt to explain away the trend in the animal behavior literature toward attributing greater cognitive sophistication to non-human animals. One source of this trend, she claims, is

> the outpouring of field studies on primates that began about 30 years ago. The complex social relationships among monkeys and apes, coupled with the fact that they look so much like us, seem to compel explanations of their behavior in terms of conscious thought and awareness. Maybe bees, birds, bats, fish or snakes don't think or know what they are doing, but surely apes and monkeys do.[17]

In her attempt to belittle this particular trend in the literature, Shettleworth points to the facial resemblance between monkeys and apes, on the one hand, and humans, on the other—something which everyone would agree is evidentially irrelevant to the question of cognitive sophistication—while at the same time ignoring the fact that these primates are our closest evolutionary ancestors, which one would think might have some bearing on their cognitive architecture and, accordingly, their cognitive abilities. This is a striking oversight in a book entitled *Cognition, Evolution and Behavior*.

Shettleworth goes on to dismissively cite

> a powerful human tendency to anthropomorphize other species that even professional observers of animal behavior cannot always resist. Its power is implicit in the titles of popular books like *When Elephants Weep*, *The Human Nature of Birds*, and *The Secret Life of Dogs*, and it is not the least among the factors encouraging cognitive ethologists. Understanding the behavior of other people as the expression of an underlying belief or intention is part of *folk psychology*, or plain intuitive common sense. Folk psychology is a useful predictor of other people's behavior, and it may have evolved for that reason. Generalizing to other species can be a useful informal way of predicting behavior, too. A tendency to apply folk psychology to animals could be a human adaptation for hunting and evading predators. Indeed, it is very difficult for most beginning students of animal behavior, let alone consumers of popular books, to conceive of the possibility that other species have a completely different way of understanding the world and

---

[17] Shettleworth, *Cognition, Evolution, and Behaviour*, 478.

behaving adaptively than we do. It takes a real leap of imagination to understand, for example, that a rat doesn't find its way home because it 'knows where it is' but because it is unconsciously pushed and pulled by stimuli it encounters along the way.[18]

Now there are a number of interesting things going on in this passage. That there is a, perhaps evolutionarily explained, tendency on the part of human beings to attribute intentional states to human, as well as non-human, animals is being offered as an explanation that somehow undermines the accuracy of the attributed states, at least in the case of the attributions to non-human animals. But first, why the asymmetry? Why should we accept at face value the attributions of intentional states to human beings, but reject—as nothing more than the stuff of sentimental popular literature for the gullible masses—attributions of intentional states to non-human animals? This is particularly puzzling given Shettleworth's own point that the attribution of such states is particularly useful in the prediction of the behavior of non-human animals. Normally, success in prediction and explanation is taken as evidence that a theory is at least approximately true. No doubt such folk explanation does not get all the details right. But Shettleworth is not merely suggesting that folk attribution of intentional states to non-human animals is mistaken in its details. Rather, she is suggesting that it is oversentimentalized silliness. The very point she makes in this passage seems to cut against any such view.

Now Shettleworth is surely right that non-human species often have 'a completely different way of understanding the world' than humans. But to suggest that non-human animals have a completely different way of understanding the world—that the mechanisms by which their understanding is achieved is, in many cases, quite different from ours—is altogether different from the final conclusion that she draws, that this difference in the mechanism by which understanding is achieved thereby undermines the claim that these

[18] Ibid. 478–9.

non-human animals actually know various things. If you arrive at my home by carefully and self-consciously following a map that I've drawn for you and I drive home from work without thinking about the route at all, the two of us have certainly made use of different cognitive mechanisms for getting to my home. But that hardly shows that only one of us knows how to get to my house. It certainly doesn't show that I don't know where my home is. Difference in mechanism for achieving understanding does not undermine the claim that understanding is thereby achieved.

Let us look in detail at a case in which the common-sense explanation of the behavior of a non-human animal is actually debunked, a case in which the tendencies to project folk-psychological explanations of the sort Shettleworth describes actually go wrong. I think it is important to look at such a case for a number of reasons. First, Shettleworth is just plain right in thinking that these cases are quite common. Second, just as Shettleworth herself is quite concerned not to have her work influenced by such common-sense explanations, precisely because they do so often go wrong, I believe that such a concern is widespread among comparative psychologists. But finally, the conclusion that Shettleworth draws in the above passage—that mistakes about the mechanisms by which understanding is produced thereby undermine the attribution of understanding itself—is not only mistaken, but is, in fact, a very widespread mistake in the comparative psychology literature. Indeed, it is so widespread that it deserves to be thought of as a fear of anthropomorphism.

2.5 A debunking explanation: What young chimpanzees know about seeing

A good deal of work has been done recently on cognitive development in humans that addresses the question of when children begin to attribute intentional states to others: at what point do children begin to develop a theory of mind?[19] A number of researchers have begun to address the same question with chimpanzees, with interesting results.

Casual observation of chimpanzees would lead one to believe that they do, indeed, attribute at least some intentional states to each other. Consider the case of seeing. Chimpanzees seem to recognize when other chimpanzees, and human beings as well, are attending to various phenomena. Chimps trained to request food by extending their hands toward an experimenter will request food from an experimenter who is facing them, but fail to do so when the experimenter's back is turned.[20] Such a result seems entirely unsurprising, and the obvious explanation is that the chimpanzees recognize that one experimenter is in a position to see, and thus respond to, their request, while the other is not. Such an explanation attributes quite sophisticated mental states to chimpanzees: it has the chimpanzees forming beliefs about the mental states of the experimenters. Moreover, confronted with an experimenter who is staring upward into a corner of the room, chimpanzees tend to look where the experimenter is looking,[21] which surely suggests that the chimpanzees recognize that the experimenter is looking at something and thus, once again attribute intentional states to the experimenter.

But obvious and compelling as this explanation seems, a series of subtle experiments by Povinelli and Eddy casts significant doubt on the face-value interpretation of the chimps' behavior. Confronted with one experimenter wearing a blindfold over her eyes and another experimenter wearing the same blindfold over her mouth, chimps did not beg for food significantly more often from the experimenter who could, quite clearly, see them. When one experimenter put a bucket over her head, while the other held it on her shoulders

---

[19] See e.g. Janet Wilde Astington, *The Child's Discovery of the Mind* (Harvard University Press, 1993); Alison Gopnik and Andrew Meltzoff, *Words, Thoughts, and Theories* (MIT Press, 1997).

[20] Daniel Povinelli and Timothy Eddy, 'What Young Chimpanzees Know about Seeing', *Monographs of the Society for Research in Child Development*, 61 (1996), 41.

[21] Ibid. 91.

next to her head, again, the chimps did not behave differently toward the two. There was no difference in behavior toward an experimenter who covered her eyes with her hands, and one who covered her ears with her hands.[22] Moreover, when two experimenters turned their backs to the chimps, but one looked at them over her shoulder while the other did not, the chimps again did not behave differently toward the two experimenters.[23] Quite clearly, the chimps are not responding to whether the experimenters can see them. These results run exactly counter to what one would expect were the commonsensical explanation true. Povinelli and Eddy thus conclude:

The young chimpanzees in these studies might have performed differently than they did. Instead of consistently performing according to the predictions of a model that assumed that they had no theory of mind, they could just as easily—like most of the preschoolers we tested—performed according to a different model that assumed that they had some knowledge about the relation of the eyes to an internal mental world . . . until additional data emerge to supplant those reported here, we conclude that, despite striking use of (and interest in) the eyes, 5–6-year-old chimpanzees apparently see very little behind them.[24]

Povinelli and Eddy thus provisionally reject the claim that young chimpanzees attribute intentional states to others. Instead, they offer a debunking explanation of some bits of behavior—following eye gaze and responding differentially to investigators turned toward rather than away from them—which would otherwise seem to call for an explanation involving beliefs about the intentional states of others.

Now let us assume, at least for the sake of argument, that Povinelli and Eddy are exactly right here.[25] One might think that this

---

[22] Daniel Povinelli and Timothy Eddy, 'What Young Chimpanzees Know about Seeing', *Monographs of the Society for Research in Child Development*, 61 (1996), 43.

[23] Ibid. 52.   [24] Ibid. 140.

[25] For interesting commentary largely supporting these conclusions, and, indeed, offering important additional evidence in their favor, see Michael Tomasello, 'Chimpanzee Social Cognition', *Monographs of the Society for Research in Child Development*, 61 (1996), 161–73. See also Dorothy Cheney and Robert Seyfarth, *How Monkeys See the World* (University of Chicago Press, 1990).

is precisely the sort of experimental work that would justify the attitude I labeled a 'fear of anthropomorphism'. But it is important to see just what Povinelli and Eddy are arguing for and against. While they argue that current evidence runs counter to the suggestion that chimpanzees attribute mental states to others, and thus they do not attribute second-order mental states to chimpanzees, this is not to say that Povinelli and Eddy reject the attribution of first-order mental states to chimpanzees. Indeed, quite the opposite is true. They specifically talk about what chimpanzees know and understand.[26] They take for granted that chimpanzees have first-order mental states, and, more than that, the very point of their monograph is to reject a central tenet of behavioral learning theory, that there is a single mechanism at work underlying behavioral change in all species,[27] a mechanism whose operation can accurately be described without adverting to mental states of any kind. More than this, the explanation Povinelli and Eddy offer instead of the commonsensical appeal to second-order intentional states is one that itself appeals to what chimpanzees know and understand.[28] So while Povinelli and Eddy are offering a debunking explanation for certain aspects of the behavior of young chimpanzees, they are not committed to, nor do they accept, an explanation that would, at a stroke, undermine all mentalistic explanations of chimpanzee behavior of whatever sort.

My talk of fear of anthropomorphism is thus motivated by a desire to avoid a certain sort of mistaken conclusion that one might draw from the many examples of debunking explanations, such as that of Povinelli and Eddy, found in the animal behavior literature. These debunking explanations are narrowly geared to undermine particular mentalistic hypotheses. This is a common enough feature of the animal behavior literature that investigators are rightly concerned not to assume that bits of animal behavior with salient

---

[26] See especially 'What Young Chimpanzees Know about Seeing', 16.
[27] Ibid. 4.   [28] Ibid. 16.

similarities to human behavior are explained by the same psychological mechanisms underlying the human case.[29] But when the existence of these debunking explanations is used, not to undermine particular psychological explanations and replace them with better psychological explanations, but rather to somehow cast skeptical doubt on the suggestion that there are psychological explanations for animal behavior in general—as we saw in the discussion of Shettleworth in the last section—then we have a case of what I have been calling the fear of anthropomorphism, and this is, as I have been urging, very much the wrong conclusion to draw.

Typical debunking explanations in the animal behavior literature do not replace psychological explanations with non-psychological alternatives; rather, they replace one sort of psychological explanation with another. There is no longer a serious question of whether much of animal behavior requires psychological explanation. The real questions at issue in the literature is what psychological explanations are required.

2.6 From belief to knowledge

The work of Povinelli and Eddy thus casts doubt on the claim that chimpanzees have a theory of mind, that they attribute mental states to various animals. The explanation of their behavior, however, certainly requires attributing mental states to the chimps themselves. While the chimpanzees do not beg for food from the investigator facing them rather than the one whose back is turned because they believe that one can see them while the other cannot, they do certainly recognize that one investigator is facing them while the other is not. Explaining their behavior, while it does not require the attribution of a theory of mind, does require the attribution of beliefs.

---

[29] For important work of this sort on the understanding chimpanzees have of the physical world, see Daniel Povinelli, *Folk Physics for Apes: The Chimpanzee's Theory of How the World Works* (Oxford University Press, 2000).

Nor are chimps unusual in this respect. What is unusual about chimps is that they show some behavior which is prima-facie evidence, although, as it turns out, misleading evidence, that they have second-order mental states. But evidence for the existence of beliefs in the animal world is extremely widespread, and such attribution is common in the animal behavior literature. More than this, what one sees in the animal behavior literature, and with a great deal of frequency, is talk of animal knowledge.

Consider, once again, Carolyn Ristau's work on piping plovers. Like many other birds, the plover engages in distracting behaviors to keep potential predators from finding its nest.

On some approaches of an intruder, the bird may do a gradation of broken-wing displays, which may perhaps begin with a fanning tail and gradually increase the awkwardness of walk until it has one and then both wings widely arched, fluttering, and dragging. It may then vocalize loud raucous squawks as well. The broken-wing display is usually made while the bird is moving forward along the ground, although stationary displays are also made . . . The bird presents a convincing case for being injured, and the observer often trudges hundreds of meters after the bird only to see it suddenly fly away with agility. At that point one is far from the nest or young.[30]

Now there are many ways of interpreting this behavior that would not involve attributing much, if any, knowledge to the bird. But Ristau does credit the plover, and its predators, with a good deal of knowledge. She says that plovers 'know when an intruder is potentially dangerous',[31] and she speaks of investigating 'the plover's knowledge/beliefs about its environment'.[32] A hypothesis Ristau considers, and eventually accepts, 'requires that the plover must know the location and movements or trajectories of the young and the intruders in order to respond appropriately'.[33] The plover's nest is camouflaged, thereby 'preventing potential predators' knowledge of the nest's location'.[34] Both the plovers themselves, and their predators, are seen as fit subjects of knowledge attributions.

[30] Ristau, 'Aspects of the Cognitive Ethology of . . . the Piping Plover', 94.
[31] Ibid. 105. [32] Ibid. 123. [33] Ibid. 96. [34] Ibid. 94.

Now talk of knowledge in these situation might be used colloquially, carrying little, if any, theoretical commitment. Just as we sometimes speak of an electric door opener 'knowing' whether someone is approaching, an investigator might also speak of plovers 'knowing' various things about their environment, without thereby being committed to the existence of genuine intentional states in such lowly creatures, let alone to real attributions of knowledge. This is clearly not the case, however, in Ristau's work. Indeed, the very point of Ristau's investigation of the plover's broken-wing display is to examine the extent to which intentional idioms are required in explaining such behaviors.[35] Ristau may be mistaken in claiming that the plover and its predators are genuine subjects of knowledge, but she is clearly not using these terms casually. She is fully committed to the attribution of intentional states to these animals, and offers a good deal of evidence in favor of that commitment.[36]

One might still reasonably wonder whether talk of *knowledge* is doing any work here, rather than some other, weaker, intentional idiom, in particular, talk of belief. Even if we grant that the sophistication of the plover's behavior requires the use of intentional idioms, what is it that licenses talk of genuine knowledge here, rather than the more prosaic belief? Admittedly, the plover's beliefs are, on many occasions, true, but knowledge is, surely, more than just true belief, and if a case is to be made that plovers are potential subjects of knowledge, more needs to be done than merely defend the view that they are subjects of intentional states. How big a step is it, however, from attributions of belief to attributions of knowledge?

[35] Ristau, 'Aspects of the Cognitive Ethology of . . . the Piping Plover', 93. See passage quoted from Ristau above, sect. 2.1.

[36] In particular, Ristau considers both the possibility that the broken wing display is a reflex, and, more plausibly, a fixed action pattern. The extent to which the behavior is responsive to detailed information about the environment, however, makes both these interpretations less plausible than the fully intentional reading of the birds' behavior. Ristau's discussion of the extent to which the behavior of intruders is monitored by the plover is especially relevant here.

While Ristau devotes a good deal of attention to the evidence for intentional states in plovers, she does not directly discuss the question of whether plovers have knowledge, rather than mere true belief, nor does she discuss what kind of evidence is needed to make this additional step. The fact remains, however, that she does repeatedly refer to the plover's knowledge of its environment, and this particular way of describing animals is hardly idiosyncratic. Cognitive ethologists who do not simply avoid attributions of intentional idioms across the board typically use the term 'knowledge', as Ristau does, without comment. Indeed, it is noteworthy that the use of the term 'knowledge' seems so unremarkable to these investigators, many of whom, like Ristau, are quite self-conscious in their use of intentional idioms generally. While these investigators rightly spend a good deal of time and effort in constructing and carrying out experimental tests of their commitment to the usage of intentional idioms, they seem to regard the use of the term 'knowledge' as uncontroversial, once the battle for the usage of intentional idioms has been won.[37]

Louis Herman and Palmer Morrel-Samuels[38] directly address the issue of knowledge attribution, however, in their work on dolphins.

---

[37] This passage, from Michael Tomasello and Josep Call, *Primate Cognition* (Oxford University Press, 1997), 367, is not atypical: 'In the physical domain, virtually all species studied have demonstrated a basic knowledge of permanent objects and some of the ways they may be related to one another spatially, quantitatively, and in terms of their perceptual similarities. In the social domain, virtually all species studied have demonstrated a recognition of individual groupmates and a knowledge of some of the important ways they may be related to one another socially and behaviorally. In both domains individuals have demonstrated the ability to use this knowledge to formulate various types of strategies, ranging from efficient foraging and tool use to coalition strategies and social learning, that help them attain their goals with respect to such basic adaptive functions as feeding and mating.'

[38] Louis Herman and Palmer Morrel-Samuels, 'Knowledge Acquisition and Asymmetry Between Language Comprehension and Production: Dolphins and Apes as General Models for Animals,' in M. Beckoff and D. Jamieson (eds.), *Interpretation and Explanation in the Study of Animal Behavior*, i. *Interpretation, Intentionality, and Communication* (Westview, 1990), 283–312.

Receptive competencies support knowledge acquisition, the basic building block of an intelligent system. In turn, knowledge and knowledge-acquiring abilities contribute vitally to the success of the individual in its natural world, especially if that world is socially and ecologically complex, as is the case for the bottle-nosed dolphin . . . Among the basic knowledge requisites for the adult dolphin are the geographic characteristics and physiographic characteristics of its home range; the relationships among these physical features and seasonal migratory pathways; the biota present in the environment and their relevance as prey, predator, or neutral target; the identification and integration of information received by its various senses, including that between an ensonified target and its visual representation; strategies for foraging and prey capture, both individually and in social units; the affiliative and hierarchical relationships among members of its herd; identification of individual herd members by their unique vocalization and appearance; and the interpretation of particular behaviors of herd members . . . This is undoubtedly an incomplete listing and is in part hypothetical, but is illustrative of the breadth and diversity of the knowledge base necessary to support the daily life of the individual dolphin. Similar analyses could be made of knowledge requirements of apes or of other animal species, but the underlying message is the same: extensive knowledge of the world may be required for effective functioning in that world and much of the requisite knowledge is gained through the exercise of receptive skills.   (pp. 283–4)

Herman and Morrel-Samuels suggest an interesting interpretative strategy. Knowledge attributions are essentially derivative, on their view, from attributions of receptive competencies and knowledge-acquiring abilities.[39] If an animal is to survive, it must not only be endowed with the ability passively to recognize certain features of its environment; it must also have certain strategies for active investigation of its surroundings. Information that is picked up from these receptive competencies and knowledge-gathering strategies must then be integrated to form a comprehensive understanding

[39] There is a striking similarity between this and Sosa's virtue-theoretic approach. See *Knowledge in Perspective: Selected Essays in Epistemology* (Cambridge University Press, 1991), parts III and IV, and 'Reflective Knowledge in the Best Circles', *Journal of Philosophy*, 94 (1997), 410–30.

of the animal's environment. Successful functioning in a complex environment makes various informational demands on the animal, and we must therefore view the animal's behavior as mediated by way of a system that accommodates such sophisticated information processing.

Knowledge, on this view, first enters our theoretical picture at the level of understanding of the species, rather than the individual. Explanations of individual behavior require reference to desires and beliefs, but a distinction between belief and knowledge is simply irrelevant here. If we want to explain why a particular plover left its nest and thrashed about in the open while moving away from the nest, we need only appeal to the plover's belief that a predator was nearby and approaching more closely, together with the plover's desire to protect its eggs. In explaining this behavior, it is irrelevant that the plover's beliefs happen to be true. Given that the plover has these beliefs, it would behave this way whether the beliefs were true or not.

When we turn to an explanation of the cognitive capacities of the species, however, the theoretical enterprise we are now engaged in requires more than mere belief. We are no longer interested in explaining why a particular plover moved from its nest in a way that was bound to bring the predator's attention; instead we are interested in an explanation of how it is that members of the species are endowed with a cognitive capacity that allows them successfully to negotiate their environment. It is the focus on this adaptation of these cognitive capacities to the environment that forces us to explain the possibility of successful behavior, and it is the explanation of successful behavior that requires the notion of knowledge rather than mere belief. Knowledge explains the possibility of successful behavior in an environment, which in turn explains fitness.

The suggestion here is not that the notion of knowledge does not apply to individuals; it certainly does. Rather, the suggestion is that the presence of cognitive capacities across individuals—and, in some cases, across species—is itself something that requires explanation; explanation of the presence of such cognitive capacities requires that we advert to knowledge.

Notice that these explanations require more than just the category of true belief. If we are to explain why it is that plovers are able to protect their nests, we must appeal to a capacity to recognize features of the environment, and thus the true beliefs that particular plovers acquire will be the product of a stable capacity for the production of true beliefs. The resulting true beliefs are not merely accidentally true; they are produced by a cognitive capacity that is attuned to its environment. In a word, the beliefs are reliably produced. The concept of knowledge which is of interest here thus requires reliably produced true belief.

This perspective commits us to both the following claims:

1. An animal's cognitive capacities are seen as a product of natural selection. The best explanation of the animal's cognitive capacities is that they were selected for.

2. Behavior that contributes to fitness makes certain informational demands on the animal, and the animal's cognitive capacities were selected for their ability to play this role.

Since both these claims are controversial, I want to say a bit about each of them.

The claim that an animal's cognitive capacities are best explained by natural selection is decried in some circles as crude adaptationism. Richard Lewontin, for example, denies that we know anything at all about the origins of our cognitive equipment.[40] It has rightly been pointed out from Darwin to the present day that natural selection is not the only force at work in the evolution of traits, and so it

[40] Richard Lewontin, 'The Evolution of Cognition', in D. Osherson and E. Smith (eds.), *Thinking: An Invitation to Cognitive Science* (MIT Press, 1990), iii. See also Stephen Jay Gould and R. Lewontin, 'The Spandrels of San Marcos and the Panglossian Paradigm: A Critique of the Adaptationist Programme', *Proceedings of the Royal Society of London*, 205 (1978), 281–8, and S. J. Gould and E. Vrba, 'Exaptation—A Missing Term in the Science of Form', *Paleobiology*, 8 (1982), 4–15.

is surely a hasty and unwarranted move from the existence of an arbitrary trait in some species to the conclusion that it is the product of natural selection.

While Lewontin is surely right about this point, it is worth noting that neither Lewontin nor any of the other critics of the selectionist explanation of our cognitive equipment wholly abstain from selectionist explanations of particular traits. It would be absurd to deny that lungs were selected for their role in introducing oxygen to the blood, or that hearts were selected for their role in circulation of the blood. Complex organs are universally regarded as best explained by natural selection, rather than exclusively by appeal to other forces. But the move to such an explanation of our cognitive equipment is not then a case of mindless disregard of the other forces that may be at work in evolution. As with our internal organs, our cognitive equipment is plausibly viewed as a product of selection.[41]

Our second claim—that an animal's cognitive capacities were selected for their ability to allow information about the environment to inform the animal's behavior—goes still further. What is being claimed here is that natural selection is selecting for knowledge-acquiring capacities, that is, processes of belief acquisition that tend to produce truths, and one might reasonably wonder whether this is the sort of thing for which natural selection might select. As many authors have argued, there are cases in which one process of belief acquisition is less reliable than another, and yet more conducive to survival. Faced with a choice between two such processes, natural selection will favor the more survival-conducive, and less truth-conducive, process. But then, it seems, it is conduciveness to survival that is being selected for rather than conduciveness to truth.

[41] This point is also made by Daniel Dennett, Ruth Millikan, and Edward Stein. See Dennett, 'Intentional Systems in Cognitive Ethology: The "Panglossian Paradigm" Defended', in *The Intentional Stance* (MIT Press, 1987), 237–68; Millikan, 'Propensities, Exaptations, and the Brain', in her *White Queen Psychology and Other Essays for Alice* (MIT Press, 1993), 41–4; E. Stein, *Without Good Reason: The Rationality Debate in Philosophy and Cognitive Science* (Oxford University Press, 1996), 174–86.

This argument surely proves far too much, however, for it would show that conduciveness to survival is the only thing that is ever selected for. Were we to accept this argument, we would have to deny that the shape of a carnivore's teeth are selected for their ability to rip flesh, that the shape of the panda's thumb is selected for its ability to strip bamboo leaves from the stalk, and so on. This prohibition would fly in the face of current biological practice. Biologists do speak of these traits as selected for these particular functions, in spite of the fact that the practice of carrying out these functions can at times conflict with the goal of survival, just as the practice of acquiring true beliefs can at times conflict with the goal of survival. In spite of this, it is reasonable to claim that these traits are selected for these particular functions since the animals' abilities to carry out such functions do, on the whole, enhance survivability.

Indeed, cognitive ethologists find the only way to make sense of the cognitive equipment found in animals is to treat it as an information processing system, including equipment for perception, as well as the storage and integration of information; that is, after all, the point of calling it *cognitive* equipment. That equipment that can play such a role confers a selective advantage over animals lacking such equipment no longer requires any argument. Thus, for example, John Alcock comments,

In the history of a species, some individuals with special abilities to perceive certain kinds of information around them have enjoyed relatively high success in achieving biological goals and have secured a selective advantage. As a result of natural selection the members of species of animals living today possess perceptual mechanisms that can usually be shown to be adaptive.[42]

Indeed, the very idea of animal behavior requires the reception, integration, and retention of information from a wide range of different sources. But this is just to say that any conception of sophisticated animal behavior that makes any sense of it at all will have to see the

---

[42] Alcock, *Animal Behavior*, 146.

animal's cognitive equipment as serving the goal of picking up and processing information. And this commits one to the notion of animal knowledge.

The very idea of knowledge is thus implicated in the explanation of complex animal behavior. Just as psychologists need to appeal to beliefs and desires in order to explain individual behavior, ethologists need to appeal to an animal's knowledge of its environment in order to explain fitness.

2.7 Knowledge as natural kind

I want to claim that knowledge is, in fact, a natural kind. Once we grant that cognitive ethologists are committed to the legitimacy of the category of animal knowledge, what more is involved in the claim that knowledge is a natural kind? Quite a bit, I believe. There is no available account of natural kinds that is widely agreed upon, so I will say something about what I take natural kinds to be.[43] Others may certainly disagree with part or all of this account, but the account has the advantage of at least singling out certain categories as noteworthy in virtue of features that everyone should recognize as important.

Following Richard Boyd,[44] I take natural kinds to be homeostatically clustered properties, properties that are mutually supporting and reinforcing in the face of external change. Consider the case of water. Water is just H_2O. Why does H_2O count as a natural kind? Two atoms of hydrogen and one of oxygen unite to form a homeostatic cluster. The chemical bond that joins these atoms provides the newly formed unit with a degree of stability that is not found in just any random collection of atoms. The chemical world is divided

---

[43] I develop this account in greater detail in *Inductive Inference and Its Natural Ground* (MIT Press, 1993), part I.

[44] Richard Boyd, 'How to Be a Moral Realist', in G. Sayre-McCord (ed.), *Essays on Moral Realism* (Cornell University Press, 1988), 181–228, esp. 194–9.

into kinds by nature precisely because only certain combinations of atoms yield such stable units. In the case of water, as with other natural kinds, the properties that are ultimately responsible for this homeostatic unity are also responsible for a wide range of the kind's characteristic properties. The reason natural kinds support inductive inference is that the properties that are homeostatically clustered play a significant causal role in producing such a wide range of associated properties, and in thereby explaining the kind's characteristic interactions. It is for this reason too that natural kinds feature so prominently in causal laws: laws operate over well-behaved categories of objects, and it is the homeostatic clustering of properties that explains why natural kinds are so well-behaved.[45]

Cognitive ethologists are interested in animal knowledge precisely because it defines such a well-behaved category, a category that features prominently in causal explanations, and thus in successful inductive predictions. If we wish to explain why it is that members of a species have survived, we need to appeal to the causal role of the animals' knowledge of their environment in producing behavior which allows them to succeed in fulfilling their biological needs. Such explanations provide the basis for accurate inductive inference. The knowledge that members of a species embody is the locus of a homeostatic cluster of properties: true beliefs that are reliably produced, that are instrumental in the production of behavior successful in meeting biological needs and thereby implicated in the Darwinian explanation of the selective retention of traits. The various information-processing capacities and information-gathering abilities that animals possess are attuned to the animals' environment by natural selection, and it is thus that the category of beliefs

[45] Notice that the kind of stability required for natural kindhood does not rule out those sub-atomic particles that tend to be extraordinarily evanescent. It is the clustering of certain properties that must be stable, rather than the object that has them. The possibility of reliable inductive inference requires that we can make accurate predictions about the presence of certain properties from the presence of others; it does not, on the other hand, require that the entire package of properties be long-lived. That said, it is surely the typical case that natural kinds have both sorts of stability.

that manifest such attunement—cases of knowledge—are rightly seen as a natural category, a natural kind.

2.8 Reliabilism and naturalism

The account of knowledge I am offering here is a reliability account, and it is, at the same time, a naturalistic account. Now it will probably seem unsurprising that someone favoring a reliability account of knowledge should also favor some kind of naturalism. After all, reliability theories were introduced as a means of naturalizing the theory of knowledge. But it is precisely the consistency of these two views that Robert Brandom ingeniously challenges in a recent paper.[46] I want to respond to that challenge here.

If we are to assess the reliability of a process of belief acquisition, we must specify an appropriate reference class of environments in which that process might operate, for a given process may be reliable in some environments, but unreliable in others. Thus, to take an example that Alvin Goldman made famous,[47] imagine someone looking at a barn in perfectly good light and, on the basis of his visual perception of the barn, coming to believe that there is a barn in front of him. Is this process of belief acquisition a reliable one? Intuitively, it does seem to be reliable, but whether it is genuinely reliable depends on the nature of the environment in which the perceiver is found. Thus, suppose that the area in which this particular barn is located is one in which a great many barn façades are also present; a barn façade looks exactly like a barn from the road, but, like a piece of stage scenery, it merely presents the appearance of being a barn.

---

[46] Robert Brandom, 'Insights and Blindspots of Reliabilism', *Monist*, 81 (1998), 371–92 and ch. 3 of Brandom's *Articulating Reasons: An Introduction to Inferentialism* (Harvard University Press, 2000). Page numbering refers to the original paper in the *Monist*.

[47] Alvin Goldman, 'Discrimination and Perceptual Knowledge', repr. in *Liaisons: Philosophy Meets the Cognitive and Social Sciences* (MIT Press, 1992). Goldman credits the example to Carl Ginet.

If our perceiver could not, from his vantage point, tell the difference between a barn façade and a barn, then the process by which his belief was produced would tend to produce a great many false beliefs in this particular environment; and thus, the process would not be reliable *relative to this environment*. In a different environment, of course, the very same process type would tend to produce true beliefs, and would thus be reliable *relative to those environments*. Goldman concludes that reliability must be assessed relative to an environment.

Now this, Brandom argues, is where the problem arises for those of a naturalistic turn of mind. There is nothing in the world, Brandom argues, that serves to specify the reference class against which reliability is to be assessed. Thus, for example, Brandom asks us to consider a case where our subject is, once again, looking at a genuine barn, but the barn is surrounded by barn façades. We may imagine that in this particular town, barn façades vastly outnumber real barns. But now suppose that this town is in a county in which barn façades are vastly outnumbered by real barns. And we may further suppose that this county is in a state in which real barns are vastly outnumbered by barn façades. Our reference classes alternate in the relative predominance of barns and barn façades. Our judgment about the reliability of the process producing this particular belief will clearly depend on the reference class against which we test it. But more than this, this particular example seems to illustrate the interest-relativity of our choice of reference class. Which reference class is chosen in determining the reliability of the process of belief acquisition, and thus, in determining whether our subject is said to know that there is a barn before him, cannot be found in the natural environment itself. The category of knowledge is thus not to be found out in the world; it is rather something that we impose upon it. Brandom thus uses this example to argue against a certain sort of naturalistic account of knowledge, and thereby to motivate his own account, which sees knowledge as fundamentally connected to the social practice of offering and asking for reasons.

Now I should point out right away that this particular challenge does not face everyone who defends a naturalistic theory of knowledge. In particular, the sort of account of knowledge that Alvin Goldman himself defends is in no way at odds with the suggestions Brandom makes. Goldman does not see the category of knowledge as a natural kind; he does not regard knowledge as a natural phenomenon, somehow given by the world.[48] There is nothing in Goldman's view that commits him to denying that knowledge is some kind of social construct. So Goldman's reliabilism fits perfectly well with the kind of naturalism he favors.

The view I favor, however, is just the sort that Brandom's example is meant to challenge, for I do believe that knowledge is a natural kind, and so I am committed to the view that there is a right choice of reference class, and that this is somehow determined by the world, rather than merely by our more parochial interests. Thus, unlike Goldman, I do need to respond to Brandom's challenge.

Now one way of construing the challenge Brandom presents is as a challenge in principle to the very idea of there being some privileged reference class that is determined by the world itself, rather than imposed upon it by human interests and practices. And if this is the right way to interpret Brandom's challenge, then I think that there is a fairly quick and effective response to it. Knowledge is an ecological kind: it has to do with the fit between an organism and its environment. The very idea that there should be some privileged specification of an animal's environment is not something that I am inventing qua epistemologist. Rather, the current practice of biology requires that we understand the evolutionary history of animal species as determined, in part, by adaptations to their environment, where the notion of environment is not given in any way by human interests or practices. Current biological theorizing thus requires the very specification of an environment independent of

---

[48] Indeed, he explicitly rejects this view. See Alvin Goldman and Joel Pust, 'Philosophical Theory and Intuitional Evidence', in M. DePaul and W. Ramsey (eds.), *Rethinking Intuition* (Rowman & Littlefield, 1998).

human interests which the Brandom argument says we can't have. A priori arguments against the possibility of practices that are well entrenched in successful sciences have a sad history. We would do well to side with the biologists here. If the notion of knowledge as a natural kind is no more controversial than Darwin's theory of natural selection, then it is in very good shape indeed.

But I think that this way of reading the challenge about the specification of a reference class may be unfair to Brandom. Instead of reading it as an objection in principle to the idea of nature determining a reference class, we may read the challenge differently. Biology may give us a way of fixing the notion of an animal's environment, but the question before us is whether this way of specifying a reference class gives us a recognizable notion of knowledge. In the case of non-human animals, the environment in which a process of belief acquisition must tend to produce true beliefs if the resulting beliefs are to count as knowledge is plausibly viewed as the piece of territory that cognitive ethologists would identify as the animal's natural range. But in the human case, it is not so clear that the biological notion of territory or environment properly does the job for attributions of knowledge. What Brandom's example illustrates is that there are ways of cutting up the human environment that answer to human interests and concerns, rather than biological ones, and our knowledge attributions may well be based on these various interest-relative classifications. When we attribute knowledge to an individual, we have in mind, implicitly, a certain specification of the environments in which that individual's beliefs might be reliably formed, and we simply do not care about the way a proper biology or cognitive ethology would treat the human environment. There may well be a scientific notion of knowledge that serves the purposes of biology, but there is also an everyday notion of knowledge that is answerable only to human interests, and it is this latter notion that is of interest to philosophers.

Why should we think that our everyday attributions of knowledge are informed by a specification of reference class that is somehow different from the one to which cognitive ethologists are committed? One reason might be that the barn façade example that Brandom constructs shows that there may, at times, be a kind of arbitrariness in the choice of reference class that biology does not permit. Biology does not care about the boundaries of towns, counties, and states, but we sometimes do. Because our concerns may vary, even when the biological facts do not, we may sometimes choose one reference class for our knowledge attributions, and at other times make a different choice; but biology does not ever leave things open in this way. Everyday knowledge attributions allow a degree of flexibility in the choice of reference class that biology does not allow.

Now I don't think that this objection is successful. The suggestion that the notion of environment in biology is fully determinate seems to me to be just mistaken. Consider Brandom's barn façade example. As Brandom himself notes, 'the case described is exceptional in many ways. Not every cognitive situation admits of descriptions in terms of nested, equally natural reference classes that generate alternating verdicts of reliability and unreliability . . . But situations with the structure of the barn facade example can arise . . .' Now it is surely a great understatement to say that 'not every cognitive situation admits of descriptions in terms of nested, equally natural reference classes that generate alternating verdicts of reliability and unreliability'; such highly contrived situations are, at best, rare. But Brandom is quite correct in saying that they can arise; indeed, given lumber and tools, we could go out and create such a situation right now. But notice that we can create such a situation in the biological world as well. Cognitive ethologists might sometimes use decoys and imitation predators in order more easily to view the reaction of some animal.[49] Rather than wait for a fox to come along,

---

[49] See the experimental design, for example, in Peter Mailer, Stephen Karkahian, and Marcel Gyger, 'Do Animals Have the Option of Withholding Signals When Communication is Inappropriate? The Audience Effect', in C. Ristau (ed.), *Cognitive Ethology*, 187–208.

they might put out a stuffed fox in a field and see what happens. But now we can create just the kind of environments for animals that Brandom's barn façade case imagines, and we might ask ourselves whether a particular bird, on looking at a genuine fox in a field full of fox imitations, knows that the object before it is a fox. More than this, we might place these imitation foxes in nested circles, as in Brandom's example, and leave them there over a period of millions of generations, in order to see what effect this has on natural selection.

How would biologists determine the boundaries of an animal's environment in such contrived situations? I don't believe that there is a unique and determinate answer to such a question. The biologist's notion of environment is able to do theoretical work precisely because these kinds of contrived situations do not naturally arise. Actual environments typically show changes that are more nearly continuous than those of the nested circles environment. When changes in the environment are discontinuous, these dramatic changes typically involve multiple interrelated features—terrain, vegetation, water supply, other animals, etc.—that jointly influence the behavior and range of the animals who inhabit it. If we try to extend the biologists' notion of environment to cover the highly contrived and artificial cases that we might construct, then, not surprisingly, we will be faced with a range of choices which are, to some extent, arbitrary. But the biologists' notion of environment is not in any way defective as a result of this; nor is it thereby shown to be any less of a natural kind.

I want to say the very same thing about Brandom's concentric circles of barn façades. We can contrive cases in which the choice of reference class will be arbitrary, and then, of course, the gap that nature leaves in our notion of knowledge will be filled in by human interests and concerns. But these cases are relatively rare, and this should not make us view the very idea of knowledge as any less a natural kind for all of that. What Brandom would need to show in order to undermine the idea of knowledge as a natural kind is more than that we can construct cases that defy any sort of natural classification. It would need to be shown that at least many of the kinds of cases of knowledge that are of real philosophical interest do not lend themselves to a naturalistic specification of the environment relative to which a process of belief acquisition should be counted reliable or unreliable. The barn façade case does not do that work.

2.9 Conclusion

I have argued that cognitive ethologists are committed not only to attributing beliefs to animals, but to talk of animal knowledge as well. Knowledge is a robust category in the ethology literature; it is more than belief, and more than true belief. It requires reliably produced true belief. Understood in this way, knowledge is properly viewed as a natural kind.

3

Knowledge and Social Practices

ACCOUNTS of knowledge in the recent philosophical literature may be divided into two broad types: there are those that require nothing more than a certain responsiveness to features of the environment, such as reliability accounts, tracking accounts, and the like; and there are those that require a high degree of sophisticated meta-cognitive processing. The second sort may in turn be divided into two sub-types: those that require some kind of individual metacognition, i.e. some sort of reflection on the epistemic status of one's beliefs; and those that require some kind of social metacognition, typically in the form of engagement in the social practice of giving and asking for reasons. If metacognitive processing is to be required for the possession of knowledge, whether the mandated metacognitive processes are seen as individual or social, accounts of this sort are quickly seen to have the consequence that young children and non-human animals, and often many adults as well, are incapable of achieving knowledge. And this is a result that most people find highly counterintuitive. As a result, a number of philosophers now draw a distinction. There is 'mere animal knowledge', which requires no more than responsiveness to the environment, and there is human knowledge, the philosophically interesting sort, which requires engagement in high-grade metacognition.

Thus, although Ernest Sosa defends an account of knowledge that requires sophisticated reflection on the degree of coherence of one's body of beliefs, he comments, 'This is not to deny that there is a kind of "animal knowledge" untouched by broad coherence. It is rather only to affirm that beyond "animal knowledge" there is a better knowledge. This reflective knowledge does require broad coherence, including one's ability to place one's first-level knowledge in epistemic perspective.'[1]

And Keith Lehrer comments,

Now if someone says that some animal or child knows things even though they are incapable of using what they know in reasoning and justification, I am inclined to argue and have argued that they are wrong and this is not knowledge at all. My fundamental reason is that though they may possess the information that p, they do not know that the information they possess is correct. Moreover, if they do not know that the information that they possess is correct, then they do not know that p . . . Whatever the merits of this argument . . . I now think that more clarity would result from simply saying that I am concerned with discursive knowledge which is another sort of knowledge than the primitive knowledge young children and animals possess . . .[2]

A position that is, in important respects, more extreme, is defended by Colin McGinn:

many animals that can be said to see, hear, smell, etc., what is going on around them could not literally be credited with beliefs. Such animals can, it is true, be credited with informational states that are, if you like, *analogous*

[1] Ernest Sosa, 'Reflective Knowledge in the Best Circles', *Journal of Philosophy*, 94 (1997), 422.
[2] Keith Lehrer, 'Discursive Knowledge', *Philosophy and Phenomenological Research*, 60 (2000), 638.

to genuine belief; but processing information about the environment is not the same thing as reasoning about it. So both perception and knowledge are, in a clear sense, more primitive than belief; they require less cognitive sophistication than belief.[3]

This would seem to suggest a view on which animals *do* enjoy knowledge just as much as humans, and that when humans know, what is required for them to have knowledge is no different from what is required of non-human animals. But McGinn professes attraction to a different view, a view on which the requirements for human knowledge are higher than those for, as he puts it, 'subrational animal knowledge'.[4] Once again, human knowledge and animal knowledge are said to be different in kind.

Now I don't think that human knowledge and the knowledge of children, or non-human animals, are different in kind at all. And I recognize that it may well seem quarrelsome on my part to raise this issue. After all, many, though not all, of the philosophers who draw a distinction between human knowledge and whatever it is that children and non-human animals have, are willing to grant that non-human animals have knowledge, or at least something analogous to it.[5] And surely, it will seem, this ought to be enough for any reasonable person. What difference does it make whether we talk about non-human animals knowing things in the very same sense of the term that adult human beings do?

[3] Colin McGinn, 'The Concept of Knowledge', *Midwest Studies in Philosophy*, 9 (1984), 547.

[4] The reference to 'subrational animal knowledge' is found ibid. 548; the view about human knowledge is proposed ibid. 549.

[5] It is interesting to compare the contemporary debate on this issue to the debate among the ancient Greeks on the same questions. As Richard Sorabji points out, the claim that non-human animals lack belief and reason was well represented among the ancients, especially in Aristotle and the Stoics. As Sorabji puts it, 'To compensate for the denial of reason and belief to animals, perceptual content must be expanded' (*Animal Minds and Human Morals: The Origins of the Western Debate* (Cornell University Press, 1993), 17). This, in turn, leads to the attribution of contentful states, and in some cases, 'analogues of belief' (ibid. 28) Moreover, on at least one interpretation, the Stoics insist on linguistic ability as a precondition for conceptualization, reason, and belief (ibid. 22).

But it does make a difference. We may draw a distinction, if we like, between the knowledge that residents of Vermont have—call it Vermont-knowledge—and a kind of cognitive state that may be enjoyed even by those who do not have the pleasure of living in Vermont. After all, even those who reside outside Vermont have cognitive states that are responsive to features of their environment, and they do, at times, engage in both individual and social metacognition, and so their states are at least *analogous* to Vermont-knowledge. So there is a perfectly well-defined distinction between Vermont-knowledge and mere out-of-state knowledge. Who could object to drawing such a distinction?

We should all, of course, object to drawing such a distinction, for although it is perfectly well-defined, it is a distinction that marks no significant difference. And the question at issue between those who divide human knowledge from 'mere animal knowledge', as it is so often put, is whether the two differ in kind, or whether this too is a distinction without a significant difference. I do not, of course, say a distinction without any difference. There are, without a doubt, differences between the knowledge that adult humans have and the knowledge had by children and non-human animals. But there are differences too between Vermont-knowledge and mere out-of-state knowledge. What we should want to know, before signing on to a distinction between human knowledge and mere animal knowledge, is what reason there is to think that these two are different in kind; that is, what reason there is to think that there is some real, substantive difference here, rather than a merely arbitrary difference, one that our new terminology treats as if it were significant when in fact it is not.

As I mentioned, those who give accounts of knowledge that make genuine knowledge unavailable to non-human animals fall into two groups: there are those, influenced by Descartes, who see knowledge as requiring processes of reflection that are available only to adult human beings; and there are those, often under the influence of the later Wittgenstein, and also Sellars, who see knowledge as requiring certain social practices, practices of giving and asking for reasons, that are available only to humans of a certain level of cognitive maturity. In this chapter, I take on the second group; in Ch. 4, I will consider the first.

Although the social practice of giving and asking for reasons can, at times, be quite useful in gaining knowledge, it is, to my mind, vastly overrated, and not only by philosophers who make it a prerequisite for knowledge. Giving and asking for reasons is quite often epiphenomenal with respect to the fixation of belief; it is, under many conditions, counterproductive to the acquisition of knowledge. It is not an epistemic good in and of itself; rather, it is good only given certain background conditions. Moreover, once one understands just when engagement in this particular practice is an epistemic good, it no longer looks like an independent condition on knowledge, or on belief. Instead, it seems to be a special case of other conditions on knowledge that are independently well motivated. Or so I shall argue.

3.1 Belief and the practice of giving and asking for reasons

Perhaps the most radical form of the claim that animals lack knowledge is to be found in Donald Davidson and Robert Brandom. On this view, non-human animals lack knowledge because they lack beliefs. Thus, Davidson states, 'I think it is possible for an animal to have considerable learned mastery of an environment, to employ implements, solve problems, and generally perform many tasks that require memory, learning, and calculation, without ever entertaining a propositional content. I would say such an animal does not have beliefs . . .'[6] Why is it, according to Davidson, that non-human

---

[6] Donald Davidson, 'Reply to Simon J. Evnine', in Lewis Hahn (ed.), *The Philosophy of Donald Davidson* (Open Court, 1999), 309.

animals lack beliefs? Because 'a creature cannot have thoughts unless it is an interpreter of the speech of another'.[7]

Brandom sets the standards even higher.

An assertion, even if true, is not taken to express knowledge unless the one making it *understands* the claim being made. A practical grasp of the significance of making the claim is inseparable from an appreciation of its role as possible reason for other claims, and something that reasons can in turn be offered for. It is being caught up in this way in the game of giving and asking for reasons that makes a performance the undertaking of a commitment (the making of a claim) in the first place.[8]

Non-human animals cannot have knowledge, on Brandom's view, because they do not even have beliefs; and they cannot have beliefs because they do not participate in a social practice of giving and asking for reasons.[9]

So for both Davidson and Brandom, having beliefs requires participation in a certain social practice. In the case of Davidson, it is language use: one must speak a language oneself and use it for purposes of communication; one must be 'an interpreter of the speech of another'. In the case of Brandom, it is even more than this: one must participate in the social practice of giving and asking for

---

[7] Donald Davidson, 'Thought and Talk', in *Inquiries into Truth and Interpretation* (Oxford University Press, 1984), 157.

[8] Robert Brandom, *Making It Explicit: Reasoning, Representing and Discursive Commitment* (Harvard University Press, 1994), 214.

[9] There is an even more radical view here, held by John Haugeland. On Haugeland's view there are no intentional states without what he calls 'existential commitment': 'It is the capacity for this kind of commitment that I am inclined to think is relatively recent—almost certainly more recent than language, and perhaps more recent than cities and writing. Like city-building and writing, the possibility of existential commitment is part of a cultural heritage (not just a biological or "natural" capacity)' (*Having Thought: Essays in the Metaphysics of Mind* (Harvard University Press, 1998), 2). I do not discuss this view separately, since Haugeland requires everything Brandom does, and possibly more besides, and thus if what I have to say about Brandom is correct, Haugeland's views fall for the same reason. It is perhaps worth pointing out that on Haugeland's view, it appears that many *Homo sapiens* living today in cultures that lack both cities and writing will turn out to lack intentional states of all sorts. They will not be able to 'know, want and understand things' (ibid. 2).

reasons. In both cases, not only non-human animals, but pre-linguistic infants lack beliefs. The status of children in the early stages of language use is problematic for Davidson,[10] although not for Brandom; on Brandom's view, they too lack beliefs. And finally, as we shall see, even certain adult human language users, on Brandom's view, lack beliefs as well.

Let us begin with Brandom's view. Belief requires engagement in the social practice of giving and asking for reasons. Now my own casual experience suggests that the extent to which individuals engage in this practice varies a great deal. Some individuals spend a great deal of time and effort offering reasons for their beliefs and actions, and asking for reasons from others. Many individuals are less involved in this practice. One should actually distinguish between the two sides of the practice, for they do not always go together. One might spend a great deal of time offering reasons, but little time asking for them; or one might ask for reasons a great deal, but rarely offer them oneself. But however one looks at this phenomenon, this social practice, there can be little doubt that there is tremendous individual variation. Those who are the most active participants in the practice—I will say that such individuals are highly *Socratic*—are active for a variety of reasons. Some, including some of my best friends, have a professional interest in the topic of reasons for belief and action. Others engage in the practice to an extent, and in a manner, that is highly dysfunctional; they obsess over reasons, for belief or for action, and their obsession gets in the way of forming accurate and timely beliefs and effective decisions. The two classes, of course, need not be disjoint. Similarly, those at the low end of activity here, those who are not very Socratic at all, have a variety of reasons for their limited participation in this practice. Some are merely laconic; they don't say much at all, let alone stop to offer reasons for their beliefs and actions, or question the reasons of others. And there are some who see the entire practice as

[10] See Davidson's discussion of this issue in 'Reply to Evnine'.

rude or boorish. Consider Robert Nozick's comments on what he calls 'coercive philosophy':

The terminology of philosophical art is coercive: arguments are *powerful* and best when they are *knockdown*, arguments *force* you to a conclusion, if you believe the premises you *have to* or *must* believe the conclusion, some arguments do not carry much *punch*, and so forth. A philosophical argument is an attempt to get someone to believe something, whether he wants to believe it or not. A successful argument, a strong argument, *forces* someone to a belief.[11]

Someone who views the practice of reason-giving in this way might easily avoid it as much as possible. Such a person might well view reason-giving, and asking for reasons as well, as somehow debasing, treating a person as a mere means, failing to respect another's autonomy, or somehow a sign that one regards the other as inferior. I don't endorse such views; I merely mean to point out that some people do, in fact, regard the practice of giving and asking for reasons in this way.

As a result of these individual differences, one may rank individuals by the extent to which they engage in the practice of giving and asking for reasons, with those who simply avoid it altogether at one end, and those who hardly venture an opinion without offering an argument in its favor, or hear an opinion from another without asking for its ground, at the other end. And it wouldn't be surprising if there were substantial cultural differences here as well, with some cultures ranking high on the Socratic scale, and others, perhaps because they view the practice as rude or boorish, ranking rather low. Brandom would clearly regard those who are highly Socratic as,

[11] Robert Nozick, *Philosophical Explanations* (Harvard University Press, 1981), 4. Similarly, David Lewis remarks, 'The reader in search of knock-down arguments in favor of my theories will go away disappointed. Whether or not it would be nice to knock disagreeing philosophers down by sheer force of argument, it cannot be done.' And in a footnote on this passage, he comments, 'It would not be nice, of course. Robert Nozick has drawn attention to our strange way of talking about philosophical argument as if its goal were to subjugate the minds of our esteemed colleagues, and to escape their efforts to do likewise to us' (*Philosophical Papers*, (Oxford University Press, 1983), i. p. x).

without a doubt, genuine believers. And those who fail to engage in the practice at all, by his criterion, simply fail to have beliefs. This is, at a minimum, highly counterintuitive.

More than this, there is the question of just how much of the Socratic practice one must engage in if one is to count as genuinely having beliefs. Someone who never gives or asks for reasons, and is part of a culture that simply opts out of the practice, does not have beliefs at all. But Brandom might either hold that having beliefs is a matter of degree, where the degree to which one counts as a genuine believer corresponds to one's rating on the Socratic scale; or, alternatively, he might hold that there is some threshold, some point on the scale, perhaps a three or a four on a scale of one to ten, such that those below that point simply lack beliefs and those above it have them. Brandom does not address the question of how much one must engage in this practice to count as a believer, but it seems to me that it should actually be an important theoretical question for him. If failing to engage in the practice at all means that one is utterly lacking in beliefs, then could offering reasons for a belief on a single occasion be enough to vault oneself into the ranks of intentional beings? Some theoretically motivated view is required here.

It is not just that the concept of belief with which Brandom is operating is not our ordinary concept of belief. If our ordinary concept is somehow defective, we should welcome conceptual revision. But where is the defect in our ordinary concept that shows it to be in need of correction? Consider, for example, how it is that we would normally explain the great variation in the extent of participation in the social practice of reason-giving. Some individuals view the practice as an extremely useful one, a practice that enables them to form more accurate beliefs and more effective decisions. They ask others for reasons, not because they regard these others as inferiors; quite the opposite, to ask for reasons can be a show of respect, a sign that one takes for granted that there must be a reason behind the other's opinion or action, and the enquiry after reasons is aimed at informing the questioner, rather than berating the person questioned.

But this is not the only reason one might engage in the practice. Some do use the practice of reason-giving as a weapon, flaunting their superior argumentative abilities in ways that demean those who are subjected to it. They act like schoolyard bullies, but use words rather than sticks and stones. They are active participants in the practice of giving and asking for reasons—genuine believers on Brandom's criterion—but their motivation for engaging in the practice leaves something to be desired.

Note that these two common-sense explanations appeal to an interaction between an individual's beliefs and desires in order to explain that individual's actions, surely a common explanatory strategy. In this case, the actions explained are the very practices that Brandom makes a precondition for having beliefs: the practice of giving and asking for reasons. Moreover, there are equally good belief and desire explanations for those at the low end of the Socratic scale: for example the laconic, as well as those who regard the whole practice, for whatever good or bad reasons, as demeaning. Their actions too are explained by their beliefs and desires. Their failure to participate in the practice of giving and asking for reasons seems to have an obvious explanation in their intentional states, just like those at the high end of the Socratic scale.

Brandom notes that 'The possibility of extracting information from the remarks of others is one of the main points of the practice of assertion, and of attributing beliefs to others.'[12] This may well be right. But it is only one of the points of the practice of attributing beliefs to others; and surely a central point has to do with the role of belief in explaining behavior. More than this, the possibility of extracting information from the remarks of others is dependent upon the role of belief in explaining behavior. It is only because people so frequently assert claims that they believe, and that the claims that they believe are so often true, that assertion may play a role in transmitting information from one individual to another. But

[12] Robert Brandom, 'Insights and Blindspots of Reliabilism', Monist, 81 (1998), 389.

understanding assertion as a product of underlying belief, under certain conditions, is merely a special case of understanding action as a product of beliefs and desires. The possibility of transmitting information is thus not the sole purpose of belief attribution, nor is it the most fundamental.

We cannot make sense of the linguistic behavior of individuals, however much they may or may not engage in the practice of giving and asking for reasons, without making reference to their beliefs and desires. Giving and asking for reasons is not a prerequisite for having beliefs; it is, instead, a product of having beliefs. We explain the behavior of non-human animals, pre-linguistic infants, young children, and laconic Yankees by appeal to their beliefs and desires; we cannot make sense of their behavior otherwise. Even in the case of active participants in the practice of giving and asking for reasons, we make sense of their participation in that practice by seeing it as a means to desire fulfillment. Just as Putnam's Superspartans[13] made clear that the connection between pain behavior and pain is causal and not constitutive, laconic Yankees—or perhaps, Superyankees, a community of individuals who never in their lives either give or ask for reasons—show that the connection between belief and the practice of giving and asking for reasons is also causal and not constitutive.

Now perhaps I have been reading too much into Brandom's talk of 'the social practice of giving and asking for reasons'. While Brandom frequently speaks of this social practice as a prerequisite for belief, he sometimes seems to equate it with something else, or at least, with a standard that seems to be quite different and far less demanding. Thus, Brandom says that 'Practitioners who can produce and consume assertions are *linguistic* beings. Practitioners who can produce and consume reasons are *rational* beings. Practitioners who can produce and consume knowledge claims are *cognitive*

[13] Hilary Putnam, 'Brains and Behavior', in *Mind, Language and Reality: Philosophical Papers* (Cambridge University Press, 1975), i. 325–41.

beings. On the account presented here, these are three ways of talking about the same practices and the same capacities.'[14] Now it is one thing to claim that knowledge requires the having of reasons; I certainly would not want to disagree with that. And surely rational beings are ones who are capable of being moved by reasons; we can call this, following Brandom, 'being a consumer of reasons'. But Brandom runs together the capacity to be moved by reason with the capacity to produce reasons, thereby making more plausible the suggestion that having reasons is, or requires, linguistic capacity. And having run together these two capacities, he goes on to run together the practices corresponding to these capacities. But as we have seen, it is surely implausible to suggest that the practice of speaking a language should simply be *identified* with the practice of giving and asking for reasons. And it is also a mistake to suggest that having and being moved by reasons should be equated with being in a position to articulate them. It is a further mistake to suggest that anyone who is in a position to articulate his reasons will thereby participate in such a practice.

If Brandom weakens his requirements on belief to include nothing more than speaking a language, then his position reduces to Davidson's, a position I will turn to shortly. But if the requirement of participating in the social practice of giving and asking for reasons is taken at face value, then the suggestion that it is a necessary condition for having beliefs loses all plausibility. At one point, Brandom indicates that the various requirements he lays down are meant to distinguish beliefs from other representations,[15] and so he is led to a position in which, it seems, it may now be granted that non-human animals, young children, and those who are at the low end of the Socratic spectrum actually do have mental representations, but do not have beliefs. While this kind of move does allow for an explanation of the behavior of these subjects, something which would not

---

[14] Brandom, *Making It Explicit*, 203.
[15] Brandom, 'Insights and Blindspots of Reliabilism', 391.

be possible without it, one is left wondering whether there is any real difference left between those who say that these creatures do actually have beliefs and the position Brandom is finally left endorsing. After all, if Brandom is content to attribute representational states that are responsive in sophisticated ways to features of the environment and that interact with other representational states that are responsive to the various animals' needs, and these two different kinds of states jointly conspire to produce action, then he has surely given up the game. One can refuse to call these states 'beliefs' and 'desires', but the philosophical content that such a denial might have had has now been drained from the claim.

Brandom's distinctive social requirements on believing are often couched in terms of his insistence that believers be 'scorekeepers' in the 'game' of giving and asking for reasons.[16] But what it takes to be a scorekeeper is not entirely clear. At times, the requirements are extremely restrictive: they require participation in the social practice of giving and asking for reasons, or at least, being part of a community that does so. For example, Brandom claims that

A community precluded from giving reasons for beliefs cannot so much as have the concept of reliability—nor, accordingly, (by anyone's lights) of knowledge. Its members can serve as measuring instruments—that is, reliable indicators—both of perceptible environing states, and of each other's responses. But they cannot treat themselves or each other as doing that. For they do not discriminate between reliable indication and unreliable indication.[17]

But first, it is entirely unclear that those who are not part of a community that gives and asks for reasons cannot have the concept of reliability. My Superyankees never give or ask for reasons, but that does not mean that they trust everyone equally. They may well recognize that some individuals are quite reliable, while others are entirely untrustworthy; they just don't talk about it. They may

---

[16] See Brandom, *Making It Explicit*, 199–229, *passim*, and 'Insights and Blindspots of Reliabilism'.　　　　[17] Brandom, 'Insights and Blindspots of Reliabilism', 379.

certainly have the concept of reliability, and self-consciously bring it to bear on what others say. They don't give or ask for reasons; but they have the concept of reasons, and they make use of it. They surely discriminate between reliable and unreliable indication. And if scorekeeping amounts to nothing more than that—being able to discriminate between reliable indicators and unreliable ones—then many non-human animals are certainly scorekeepers in this less restrictive sense, for they demonstrably learn. Pigeons pecking at colored disks are able to discriminate between reliable and unreliable indicators of food. They don't self-consciously bring to bear a concept of reasons, but that isn't required for discriminating between reliable and unreliable indication. This less restrictive sense of 'being a scorekeeper' may well be a requirement on believing, but it not only doesn't require giving and asking for reasons; it doesn't require having a language, and it doesn't require any sort of social practice at all.

I conclude that Brandom gives us no reason at all to think that participating in the social practice of giving and asking for reasons, or being part of a community that does so, is a requirement on belief.[18] If there are social prerequisites of belief, we will have to look for them elsewhere.

3.2 Belief and language use

So let us turn to Davidson's view, the view that one must be a language user in order to have beliefs.[19] One must, on Davidson's view, both use and interpret the speech of others: 'only creatures with speech', Davidson says, 'have thoughts'.[20] The result, and a result

---

[18] My conclusions here make a number of points of contact with remarks of Allan Gibbard in his 'Thought, Norms, and Discursive Practice: Commentary on Robert Brandom, *Making It Explicit*', *Philosophy and Phenomenological Research*, 56 (1996), 715–17.

[19] One also finds related arguments in Daniel Dennett, *Content and Consciousness* (Routledge & Kegan Paul, 1969).   [20] Davidson, 'Thought and Talk', 167.

that Davidson embraces, is that non-human animals and pre-linguistic infants do not have any knowledge whatsoever, and they do not have knowledge because they do not have beliefs.

Why should we believe this? Davidson does acknowledge that the 'natural reaction'[21] to the question 'can languageless animals have beliefs?' is that they can. Davidson himself gives this example: 'there is Norman Malcolm's dog who, having chased a squirrel into the woods, barks up the wrong tree. It is not hard to credit the dog with the belief that the squirrel is in that tree.'[22] It is, I think, revealing that Davidson need not appeal here to sophisticated experimentation in the animal behavior literature. The case in favor of animal belief surely seems to be overwhelming, the evidence for it ubiquitous. At the same time, Davidson also pooh-poohs the evidence. 'Attributions of intentions and beliefs to dogs smack of anthropomorphism,' he says;[23] 'fond parents', we are told, 'go to great lengths to make sage sense of their children's cooing'.[24] A certain argument Davidson makes against attributing beliefs to animals is one that he says, 'will probably be less persuasive to dog lovers than to others'.[25] One gets the impression that Davidson regards those who do, in fact, attribute beliefs to languageless creatures as, at best, naïve. But what then is the reason for withholding such attributions?

Davidson offers a number of considerations. First, when we attribute beliefs on the basis of non-linguistic behavior alone, there is a problem of underdetermination.

What is certain is that all the standard ways of testing theories of decision or preference under uncertainty rely on the use of language. It is relatively simple to eliminate the necessity for verbal responses on the part of the subject: he can be taken to have expressed a preference by taking action, by moving directly to achieve his end, rather than by saying what he wants. But this cannot settle the question of what he has chosen. A man who takes an apple rather than a pear when offered both may be

---

[21] Davidson, 'Thought and Talk', 155.   [22] Ibid.
[23] Ibid.   [24] Davidson, 'Reply to Simon J. Evnine', 305.
[25] Davidson, 'Thought and Talk', 164.

expressing a preference for what is on his left rather than his right, what is red rather than yellow, what is seen first, or judged more expensive.[26] If we persist in attributing desires, beliefs or other attitudes under these conditions, our attributions and consequent explanations will be seriously underdetermined.[27]

Now Davidson is surely right that the non-verbal behavioral evidence underdetermines any claim about a subject's beliefs and desires, and in this sense, non-verbal behavioral evidence 'cannot settle the question'. But first, in this sense, no theoretical claim is ever 'settled' by data, for we always have only finitely many data points and the theoretical claims we make have infinitely many observational implications. Second, and as a consequence of this first point, adding the evidence of linguistic behavior will not change this situation. Attributions of belief and desire are underdetermined by all the speech behavior we will ever see as well. And it won't help if we add in the speech behavior of the subject's linguistic community either. We will always have only a finite amount of data, with the result that our theoretical claims are always 'seriously underdetermined'. This marks no difference whatsoever between the attribution of beliefs and desires to languageless animals and the attribution of these states to the linguistically sophisticated. Davidson is arguing for an asymmetry claim—we should attribute beliefs and desires to creatures who do speak a language but not to those who do not—but claims about both sorts of creatures are underdetermined by all the evidence we will ever have. There is no asymmetry here.

I don't mean to be suggesting that we should therefore be skeptical. Each of the hypotheses that Davidson mentions—that the subject prefers objects on the left to those on the right, that he prefers red things to yellow, things seen first, or judged to be more expensive—are susceptible to experimental test, and they can be tested with or without using speech behavior. We often have reason

[26] Ibid. 162–3.   [27] Ibid. 164.

to take certain alternative hypotheses seriously and, by the same token, ignore others. I do not believe that we should be skeptical in these situations at all, and neither does Davidson. My point is simply that underdetermination by itself cannot be used to support a selective skepticism; it either washes away all theoretical claims or none.

Davidson does suggest that language use may do certain work that behavioral evidence apart from language use may not.

without speech we cannot make the fine distinctions between thoughts that are essential to the explanations we can sometimes confidently supply . . . The dog, we say, knows that its master is home. But does it know that Mr. Smith (who is his master), or that the president of the bank (who is that same master), is home? We have no real idea how to settle, or make sense of, these questions.[28]

But of course we do know how both to make sense of and to settle these questions. The dog does not know that the bank president is home. It is perfectly clear that dogs do not know what banks are and they do not know what presidents are and if anyone seriously doubts this we can show that they cannot even begin to make the relevant discriminations. As far as whether the dog knows that his master is Mr Smith, or more generally, whether dogs know the names of any individuals, we can certainly design tests to see whether they are capable of identifying individuals by name. They respond to a fairly wide range of commands; they might well be taught to recognize individuals by name. This is a matter that can be resolved straightforwardly.

A related worry—and perhaps this is part of what is on Davidson's mind here—is that the attempt to capture animal beliefs in English always seems, at best, only an approximation. If we attribute the belief that there is a squirrel in the tree to my son or daughter, we can reasonably expect that he or she will have a large number of related beliefs as well; but in the case of animals, many of these beliefs are unlikely to be within the animal's conceptual repertoire, and this in

[28] Davidson, 'Thought and Talk', 163.

turn seems to challenge the accuracy of the initial attribution. While this does, I believe, suggest that most ordinary language attributions of belief to non-human animals may, at times, be somewhat misleading, these considerations could not possibly serve to undermine the attribution of belief across the board. For note that if they did, this would equally undermine the English-language attribution of beliefs to speakers of French in cases where English-language and French-language categories do not neatly align with one another, and it would also undermine the attribution of beliefs to theoreticians with strikingly different theories from our own. If the best reason for withholding attributions of belief to non-human animals would also have us withhold attributions of belief to non-English speakers and theoreticians with views quite different from our own, then attributions of animal belief are quite secure indeed.

But Davidson explicitly acknowledges that these considerations are very far from decisive; indeed, he says that 'they do not constitute an argument'.[29] And he goes on to say, 'When I say, "Jones believes that snow is white" I describe Jones's state of mind directly: it is indeed the state of mind someone is in who could honestly assert "Snow is white" if he spoke English, but that may be a state a languageless creature could also be in.'[30] This, of course, is precisely the view Davidson claims to be arguing against. So what is Davidson's reason for rejecting it? Only on the last page of 'Thought and Talk' are we given an explanation: 'We have the idea of belief only from the role of belief in the interpretation of language, for as a private attitude it is not intelligible except as an adjustment to the public norm provided by language. It follows that a creature must be a member of a speech community if it is to have the concept of belief.'[31] As we have seen in the discussion of Brandom's view, this suggestion that the concept of belief can only get its purchase by way of a connection with language seems quite implausible. One might, for all that has been said, acquire the concept of belief in an attempt to

[29] Ibid. 164.   [30] Ibid. 167.   [31] Ibid. 170.

understand the behavior of others. Something publicly observable may be necessary; but behavior will do the trick here just as much as language.

But even if we were to accept this lemma of Davidson's—that having the concept of belief is only possible for creatures who are part of a language-using community—this does not yet establish that only such creatures may have beliefs. After all, I suspect that only creatures who are part of a language-using community may have the concept of white blood cells; but this hardly shows that the blood of languageless creatures lacks such cells.

Davidson recognizes that an additional premise is required here. Here is the full text of what he says on this issue.

Can a creature have a belief if it does not have the concept of belief? It seems to me that it cannot, and for this reason. Someone cannot have a belief unless he understands the possibility of being mistaken, and this requires grasping the contrast between truth and error—true belief and false belief. But this contrast, I have argued, can emerge only in the context of interpretation, which alone forces us to the idea of an objective, public truth.[32]

Now the idea that a creature can only have beliefs if it understands the possibility of being mistaken has some initial plausibility. But there are weak and strong readings of this idea. Norman Malcolm's dog, who is found barking up the wrong tree, certainly comes to understand that it has made an error when the squirrel suddenly darts away from behind a neighboring bush. The ability to respond to mistakes and make corrections in light of them is, without doubt, a feature of animal learning. But this involves a weaker reading of 'understanding the possibility of being mistaken' than Davidson undoubtedly intends. Davidson insists that such understanding, in his stronger sense, requires 'grasping the contrast between truth and error', and I certainly wouldn't want to claim that languageless

---

[32] Davidson, 'Thought and Talk', 170.

animals have the concept of truth, let alone 'an objective public truth'. But the claim that having beliefs requires understanding the difference between getting things right and making a mistake is only plausible when talk of understanding here is given a fairly weak reading. Davidson gives us no reason at all to think otherwise.[33]

Neither Brandom nor Davidson succeeds in showing that the having of beliefs requires being part of a community that engages in social practices of any sort. If there is a ground for thinking that human knowledge and animal cognition differ in kind, it is not because non-human animals lack beliefs.

3.3 Knowledge and the practice of giving and asking for reasons

A far less radical, and far more defensible, position is taken here by Michael Williams. Williams does not deny that non-human animals have beliefs, but he does deny that they have knowledge: 'Epistemic rights and privileges accrue to us in virtue of induction into a linguistic community, with its shared epistemic practices. This is one reason why animals and little children don't have them. If you can't learn the game, you don't get to play.'[34] Williams focuses on the same social practices that concern Brandom: the tracking of entitlements and commitments, what Brandom calls 'scorekeeping'. And, like Brandom, Williams's requirement here has to do with being a member of the appropriate kind of linguistic community. But the work that the linguistic community does for Williams is to create a

---

[33] Simon Evnine presents an interesting and useful discussion of difficulties Davidson would have in accounting for language acquisition in 'On the Way to Language', in Lewis Hahn (ed.), *The Philosophy of Donald Davidson* (Open Court, 1999), 289–304. Colin Allen has developed a critique of Davidson which overlaps at a number of points with the criticisms presented here; see his 'Mental Content', *British Journal for the Philosophy of Science*, 43 (1992), 537–53.

[34] 'Dretske on Epistemic Entitlement', *Philosophy and Phenomenological Research*, 60 (2000), 609.

normative practice and a normative standard that would not exist without it. Roughly, beliefs can only be justified against a background of community epistemic practice. Without such a practice, there is no justification, and thus, no knowledge.

More precisely, Williams distinguishes between epistemic grounding—roughly, reliably formed belief—and epistemically responsible belief.[35] As he points out, 'ordinary talk of "justification" remains poised uneasily between' the two, but it is closer, he believes, to the notion of responsibility.[36] Knowledge requires both grounding, i.e. reliably formed belief, and responsibility. But it is this second requirement, the requirement of responsibility—often spoken of as justification—that non-human animals and young children cannot meet. It is not that these creatures are irresponsible; rather, they fail to be (full) members of the linguistic community that makes responsibility and irresponsibility possible. Those who can't learn the standards, or who haven't yet learned them, are not held responsible for meeting them. Just as there are certain minimal requirements of understanding if one is even to be tried for committing a crime, and thus held responsible for one's conduct, there are minimal requirements of epistemic engagement if one is to be held responsible for one's beliefs.

Williams may, perhaps, be understood as offering the following argument:

[35] I myself have drawn this distinction as well, and, like Williams, argued that both were required for knowledge. Although I still think that this is an important distinction, I here reject the suggestion that both are required for knowledge. My earlier position was presented in 'Justified Belief and Epistemically Responsible Action', *Philosophical Review*, 92 (1983), 33–48; 'Ever Since Descartes', *Monist*, 68 (1985), 264–76; and 'Naturalizing Rationality', in N. Garver and P. Hare (eds.), *Naturalism and Rationality* (Prometheus Books, 1986), 115–33. The distinction is also drawn by Robert Fogelin, who also claims that both are required for knowledge. See *Pyrrhonian Reflections on Knowledge and Justification* (Oxford University Press, 1994).

[36] Williams, 'Dretske on Epistemic Entitlement', 608; Williams also discusses this view in the Afterword to *Groundless Belief: An Essay on the Possibility of Epistemology*, 2nd edn. (Princeton University Press, 1999), 183–201, and in far more detail in *Problems of Knowledge: A Critical Introduction to Philosophical Epistemology* (Oxford University Press, forthcoming).

(1) Knowledge requires justified, true belief.

(2) Justification cannot exist apart from membership in a community with certain social practices.

Therefore,

(3) Knowledge cannot exist apart from membership in a community with certain social practices.

While both the premises are intuitively plausible, one natural way of reading this argument makes it trade on an equivocation. Williams himself points out that ordinary usage of the term 'justification' 'remains poised uneasily between responsibility and grounding'.[37] Talk of 'justification' in premise (2) requires the reading of 'justification' as involving epistemic responsibility. But it is not clear that the most plausible version of premise (1) requires anything more than 'justification' as grounding. In particular, in so far as what is appealed to here is 'ordinary justification-talk', it is clearly true, as Williams suggests, that we do not talk of non-human animals as justified, or unjustified, in their beliefs; and arguably the same is true of young children. But if ordinary justification-talk is to set the standard here, then in evaluating premise (1) we should consider ordinary knowledge-talk, and it does seem that such talk makes room for the attribution of knowledge to non-human animals and children. Indeed, even those who want to argue that young children and non-human animals lack knowledge typically recognize that they are making a suggestion which, for whatever it is worth, runs contrary to most ordinary usage. Perhaps the moral here should be that knowledge requires proper grounding but not justification, at least when 'justification' is understood in the sense of epistemic responsibility. Ordinary knowledge and justification talk seem to draw a distinction between adult humans on the one hand, and non-human animals and children on the other, when it comes to justification, but not when it comes to knowledge. Note too that metaphorical

[37] Williams, 'Dretske on Epistemic Entitlement', 608.

uses of the term 'knowledge' allow attribution of 'knowledge' to various devices; for example, electric door openers are said to 'know' when someone is about to go through the door. This usage is metaphorical because the door opener does not even have beliefs; but it only makes sense at all when knowledge is seen as requiring responsiveness to the environment, and not, in addition, some kind of epistemic responsibility.[38]

But neither Williams nor I would want to place a great deal of weight on ordinary usage. What reasons are there then to suppose that knowledge cannot be had without 'induction into a linguistic community, with its shared epistemic practices'? Williams seems to hold, like Brandom, that it is these shared social practices that are the natural home of epistemic normativity. Normativity arises, on this sort of view, out of a social practice of holding people responsible for their beliefs, and it is thus only against the background of this social practice that the question of meeting or failing to meet appropriate standards even arises. Even if we bracket talk of justification for the moment, in order to avoid the problem that arose for the previous argument, it is clear that knowledge requires the meeting of certain standards. If the very existence of such standards depends on a background of social practices, then knowledge itself presupposes these social practices as well. And this will have the result, of course, that those who cannot participate in the practice, such as non-human animals and young children, thereby lack knowledge: 'If you can't learn the game, you don't get to play.'

The suggestion that the normative standards that apply to knowledge claims arise only out of shared social practices, however,

[38] Alvin Goldman makes this point in arguing for a reliabilist account of knowledge in 'Discrimination and Perceptual Knowledge', repr. in *Liaisons: Philosophy Meets the Cognitive and Social Sciences* (MIT Press, 1992). In 'What Is Justified Belief?', however (also repr. in *Liaisons*), Goldman argues for extending his reliability account to justified belief. Since this is presented by Goldman as an account of our ordinary concept, the usage point is especially relevant here. While Goldman could certainly draw on Williams's very reasonable suggestion that ordinary talk of 'justification' is ambiguous, it is noteworthy that talk of non-human animals as justified in their beliefs does seem to be simply at odds with ordinary usage.

is not clearly true. While social practices may give rise to normative commitments that would not have existed without them, they may also simply reflect normative demands that exist independently of those practices. One might think, for example, that there are good reasons for making sure that one does not drive while intoxicated even apart from the many social practices and institutions that are designed to make sure that one heeds this normative requirement. The institutions and practices reflect a social recognition of a pre-existing normative demand; they do not bring it into existence. Note, in particular, that it is hardly incoherent to suggest that a society's social practices and institutions do not adequately address a genuine responsibility that its members possess. The question to ask about the various social practices involved in giving and asking for reasons, in tracking epistemic entitlements and commitments, is whether these practices give rise to normative commitments that would not exist without them, or whether instead they are merely a reflection of the social recognition of pre-existing normative demands on belief, demands which themselves are not social in origin.

Surely not all the normative demands on belief arise socially. Even those who do not value the truth for its own sake often come to recognize that, other things being equal, the having of true beliefs is typically useful in satisfying one's desires, whatever those desires may be. And whether one realizes this or not, if it is true, there is good reason to want one's beliefs to be true, whatever else one might want. This is enough, I would claim, to generate certain normative demands on belief. I will discuss this point in more detail in Ch. 5, but all I need here is the commonsensical idea that there is some real reason to want one's beliefs to be true, the motivation for which does not derive from social practices of any sort. Even someone living alone on a desert island would have reason to favor true beliefs. More than this, the social practice of giving and asking for reasons does seem a natural outgrowth of our desire to believe truths. These practices seem to be ones that, when they are working properly, aid in the project of guiding individuals toward the truth and disseminating true belief within a culture. The cultural practices are naturally interpreted as a by-product of our independent reason to want true beliefs, not a *sine qua non* for the existence of epistemic normativity.

Indeed, note how odd it would be to suggest that there is no reason to favor true belief independent of social practices of giving and asking for reasons. If there were no normative requirements on our beliefs apart from the ones that are generated socially, then one would expect as much variation in social epistemic practice as one sees, for example, in styles of dress. Yet the striking thing about our social practice of giving and asking for reasons, of keeping track of others' entitlements and commitments, is that they all seem tied to issues of reliability. This does not seem to be a merely local cultural practice, or some widely shared and yet optional taste, like the enjoyment of sweets. The suggestion that epistemic norms would not exist without our cultural practice of giving and asking for reasons thus seems to get things backwards: we can only make sense of our social epistemic practices by seeing them as attempts to realize pre-existing epistemic norms. I will return to this theme shortly.

Let me say one more word, however, about Williams. Even if one agreed with Williams that 'learning the rules' is somehow a precondition for 'playing the game', that is, that having an understanding of epistemic norms is a precondition for being bound by them, it is a very long way from this claim to the claim that knowledge can only be had by creatures who are active members in a community that engages in fairly elaborate social epistemic practices. Williams's claim, like Brandom's, is not meant as a causal claim about the effects of socialization; they are not suggesting that the cognitive sophistication required for knowledge can only be achieved as a result of the kinds of causal interactions engaged in by highly social animals. Rather, the claim is supposed to be one about the very nature of epistemic normativity: without social practices there can be no epistemic norms. But plausible as the suggestion is that playing the game requires learning the rules, it does not suggest that there is anything essentially social about normativity. Reflective agents, even loners, might well come to the idea that not just anything goes when it comes to belief formation. Reflection on one's own past practice is often sufficient to teach this lesson. And this would thus allow one to learn the rules, and play the game, by oneself. Solitaire, too, is a rule-governed game.[39]

The attempt to see social practice as a prerequisite for knowledge, either by making it a prerequisite for belief, as do Brandom and Davidson, or by making it a prerequisite for justification, as does Williams, thus fails. Social practices may play an important role in knowledge acquisition for certain sorts of animals, in particular, for humans, but social metacognition is not a prerequisite for knowledge in animals of any sort.

3.4 Social epistemic practices, both good and bad

One striking thing about many of the philosophers who claim that social practices are a prerequisite for knowledge is that they say very little about the nature of these practices. I think it is a mistake to

---

[39] There is, famously, a large literature here on Wittgenstein's argument on rule following that is relevant to this issue. Certainly both Brandom and Williams are making arguments that are Wittgensteinian in spirit. At sect. 202 in the *Philosophical Investigations*, Wittgenstein remarks: 'Hence it is not posssible to obey a rule "privately": otherwise thinking one was obeying a rule would be the same as obeying it.' Wittgenstein's solution to this problem is to go social at this point: the normativity required for rule following is dependent on the social standards of the community. But this approach, whether in Wittgenstein, Brandom, or Williams, simply will not do. If the problem is supposed to be that an individual, acting alone, might, in principle, make mistakes in attempting to follow a rule and yet not notice them, then the same is true of a community; an entire community could make mistakes in following a rule and yet fail to notice. So if the problem is that some mistakes might, in principle, go uncorrected, the move to the community does not help. But the problem is surely not merely a practical one, and for two different reasons: first, individuals do sometimes correct themselves, so the move to the community is not always, in practice, required; and second, communities sometimes mislead individuals, and so the move to the community can, in practice, make things worse. Communities are thus, on the view presented here, one more useful but imperfect instrument for achieving desired goals, but they are not in any sense the ultimate source of normativity, let alone a precondition for the very possibility of normativity.

view the practice of giving and asking for reasons, or the practice of keeping track of epistemic entitlements and commitments, as some kind of indissoluble unity. There are many different kinds of social practice at work here, and a proper understanding of their epistemic significance can only be achieved by seeing the extent to which these practices vary. These practices are not all of a piece; they are not, in particular, all epistemically valuable.

One of the points that both Brandom and Williams make about the practice of giving and asking for reasons is that it has a 'default and challenge structure': that is, within a given epistemic community, certain claims are seen as standing in need of explicit justification, while others are taken at face value, without the need for supporting reasoning. Better still, whether the default position for a given claim is to accept it without challenge or to ask for supporting reasons depends, it is claimed, both on certain features of one's epistemic community and on the context of enquiry. This point about relativity to context of enquiry is sometimes used to defuse skeptical challenges, as when it is pointed out that in the course of chemical investigations, one might need to take seriously the challenge that one's equipment was not properly set up, but one would not need to take seriously the challenge that one was hallucinating or being deceived by a demon.[40] It is certainly true that the kinds of challenges that are likely to be presented, and the kinds of claims that are likely to be accepted at face value, vary as a function of both context and epistemic community. But once we recognize this, it is especially useful to ask how the particular default and challenge function which operates in various communities and contexts serves to aid or interfere with the project of enquiry. And the answer, of course, is that some of these epistemic practices, these default and challenge functions, are terrifically useful in directing the project of enquiry; and some of these practices are of little use at all; and still others are positively harmful.

[40] See e.g. Williams, *Unnatural Doubts: Epistemological Realism and the Basis of Skepticism* (Blackwell, 1996), 96. This kind of move was central to both the later Wittgenstein and Austin.

After all, it matters a great deal whether the claims which go largely unchallenged, in a given community and in a given context, are true or false. There are certain communities where the literal truth of the Bible is taken for granted, and so appeals to Biblical passages for guidance, in matters of morals, geology, biology, and everything else, are taken at face value and without critical examination. This has, of course, a profound effect on enquiry in these communities, and I hope I may take for granted here that the effect is, in practice, to deeply distort the beliefs of these communities and to impede enquiry on a very wide variety of subjects. The way in which these communities engage in the social practice of giving and asking for reasons deeply distorts enquiry; it distracts members of the communities from questions that would aid in getting at the truth; and it makes salient a variety of questions, for example, about the content of particular Biblical passages, which tend to lead the members of these communities to false beliefs. If a member of this kind of community could shield herself from the influence of her community on her beliefs—if she could somehow opt out of the local social practice of giving and asking for reasons— she would thereby be spared a significant source of distortion, and the attendant effect of this social isolation would be epistemically beneficial.

In many epistemic communities there is a widespread practice of deferring in a largely uncritical way to socially recognized experts; the default position on expert opinion—that is, on the position of socially recognized experts—is to accept that opinion without challenge, in the absence of specific reason to think the opinion mistaken. Indeed, so widespread is this tendency that many have argued that it is innate; and quite a few philosophers have argued, on a priori grounds, that it is epistemically justified. It is clear, however, that whether the practice has good epistemic consequences will depend on the ways in which the socially recognized experts have their special status conferred upon them, and, in particular, whether they tend to have true, or approximately true, beliefs, and whether the claims and questions on which they tend to focus public opinion serve to advance community understanding or, instead, impede it.

Consider the case of reliance on the various news media. We all rely to a very large extent on newspapers, radio, or television to inform us about current events. Clearly, the extent to which this serves to inform opinion is very much dependent on the reliability of those sources. Now it is easy enough to imagine a case of state-controlled media where citizens relying on available sources of information, and treating them with no more nor less deference than you and I treat available sources of information, will be horribly misinformed about world events. With sufficiently tight state control of information, none of the available sources of potential correctives will serve to make public opinion accurate. Cases like this, of course, are not merely imaginary. One of the effects of this kind of systematic misinformation is to play a role in determining which things come to seem obvious and in no special need of justification, and which claims require some sort of explicit justification from other available beliefs. The default position, and the claims that come to be challenged, are in part determined by the beliefs that are socially transmitted. Processes of belief acquisition and inferential tendencies that would be highly truth-conducive in other, more epistemically friendly, environments, may come to serve as vehicles of distortion and misinformation. Against the background of beliefs that such an environment creates, otherwise beneficial practices of giving and asking for reasons may come to be epistemically counterproductive. In such circumstances, one may well be far better off, epistemically speaking, if one avoids the social practice of giving and asking for reasons altogether.

Notice that the problem created by the actual practice of giving and asking for reasons, under the circumstances I have been describing, is not limited to the transmission of false belief. It is, I believe, far deeper than that. Precisely because social epistemic practices tend to focus attention on certain questions, and away from others, not only the particular beliefs transmitted, but also the entire conduct of enquiry is adversely affected. Under the pressure of particular social practices, enquiry is channeled in certain counterproductive ways. Individual inferential tendencies are bound to be affected as well, for our views and our instincts about which claims even count as good reasons for others are not immune to social influence. Those who have urged that there is an important social dimension to cognition, that social factors play a dramatic role in the acquisition, retention, and dissemination of belief, are surely correct. The role that social factors play is not always a beneficial one.

I have thus far been taking an external look at the practice of giving and asking for reasons, rather than the perspective of one of the participants in the practice. But it is one thing to show that individuals might be better off if they failed to engage in and come under the influence of the practice; it is quite another to show that they may be in a position to see that they would be better off if they failed to engage with the practice. But this second claim is true as well. Individuals may certainly be part of a society that engages in epistemically counterproductive social practices without being in a position to discover that; cases of this sort would be social analogues of evil demon cases, and sufficiently ruthless state control of information will suffice to create such a case. But it is also true that individuals may, at times, make discoveries about their society's social epistemic practices that reveal them to be significant sources of misinformation. Indeed, this happens all the time on a small scale, for example, when we discover that certain widely trusted sources of information are, in fact, unreliable. It can also occur on a much larger scale, where one discovers that, on the whole, the social epistemic practices of one's own society do more harm than good. A particularly zealous investigator of state-controlled media, in a situation where state control is, although pervasive, less than perfect, may begin to get a handle on the extent to which publicly available information is inaccurate. More than this, such an investigator may come to understand some of the adverse effects that engaging in the practice of giving and asking for reasons is likely to produce under these very circumstances. Such an investigator may then rationally decide to opt out of the social practice precisely for the purpose of insulating himself, as much as possible, from these adverse effects. While there is no guarantee that such a policy will achieve its end, neither is there any guarantee that it will fail. It may, all things considered, be the rational thing to do from the perspective of trying to improve one's epistemic situation. And under appropriate background conditions, such a policy may achieve its intended end: it may actually succeed in leading to more accurate beliefs, more epistemically productive enquiries, and more truth-conducive individual inferential tendencies.

The case of state-controlled sources of information is, of course, only one sort of case. There are other potential sources of bias in the social practice of giving and asking for reasons, and even when they are not self-consciously orchestrated by an individual or a group of individuals, as in the case of state-controlled information, they may be equally deleterious to epistemic endeavors. Feminists have rightly been concerned that, at a minimum, the public discussion of certain topics is systematically biased, and one might reasonably be concerned that this skewing of the public practice of giving and asking for reasons on these topics may have the kinds of widespread effects just enumerated: not only systematic misinformation on these topics, but the misdirection of enquiry, and the attendant distortion of individual reason. Not only Marxists, who are perhaps most famous for the claim, but members of political groups at virtually every point on the political spectrum, have argued that the character of public political discourse is horribly skewed and serves both to misinform and to interfere with, rather than enable, constructive political discourse. It has, indeed, been widely argued that the nature of much current political discussion serves to distract from important political questions and focus attention on the trivial. Under such circumstances, one may be best served, epistemically, by opting out of the public discussion. Many Washington political correspondents talk about the importance of 'getting out of the

Beltway'; the influence of public discussion within the Beltway is seen as corrupting, and, most importantly and insidiously, corrupting of individual reason. Those who remain in that environment get to a point, some hold, where they can no longer see the corrosive effects of what passes for political discourse. But this is just to say that the public practice of giving and asking for reasons is not automatically an epistemic good, nor does it present a standard against which we need to measure ourselves. In a climate where the practice of giving and asking for reasons has been badly corrupted, one need not even be able to explain, in a way that answers to public standards, why it is that one is opting out of the practice. Sometimes the right thing to do, epistemically speaking, is simply to strike out on one's own. In certain circumstances, if one wants to have knowledge, and belief worth having, one should simply stop playing the game of giving and asking for reasons, because one has come to realize that what passes for reason in the public forum is wholly alien to good epistemic practice. Meeting public standards, and engaging in the social practice of reasoning, is not a necessary condition for knowledge.

It may be pointed out that the examples I have been drawing on —feminists, Marxists, Washington political columnists—involve highly social individuals, agents who may drop out of the social practice of giving and asking for reasons, but drop out only after many years of participation. Even those who make engagement in social metacognition a prerequisite for knowledge do not require that one be so engaged at every moment, and it is certainly possible to claim that the prior social engagement is what made knowledge so much as possible for these individuals. But again, it is important to remember that the position of these philosophers is not that social engagement is a causal prerequisite for knowledge; it is supposed, instead, to be a constitutive prerequisite for knowledge. And the examples I have just been giving—the feminist, Marxist, and Washington columnist examples—work just as well if one imagines an individual who has spent his or her life on a desert island and suddenly encounters the public discourse in the environments I've described. Such an individual may reasonably wonder about what passes for reason in these environments; the public practice of reason giving may be rightly recognized for what it is, namely, a force of great destructive power, and our desert island reasoner may, just as much as our real life feminists, Marxists, and Washington correspondents, fail to engage with the public practice. Life on the desert island may be recognized for what it is: something epistemically superior to the intellectual life that results from immersion in an epistemically deviant culture. Under certain conditions, knowledge is possible only by avoiding, rather than engaging in the available social epistemic practices.

There is much to be said for engaging in the social practice of giving and asking for reasons. It can, and often does, serve a constructive epistemic purpose. But the standards set by one's community are not to be accepted uncritically. They need not be acceded to; one need not even be in a position to explain, relative to the standards of one's own community, why one will not be bound by them. Knowledge does not require engagement with the epistemic practice of any community. What is good and bad in a given social practice is best measured by the standard of reliability, a standard that may be met with or without engagement in social epistemic practices.

3.5 Conclusion

Social practices thus fail to provide a ground for distinguishing human knowledge from the knowledge of non-human animals. Language use is not essential to knowledge, nor is a social practice of giving and asking for reasons. If there is a reason to distinguish between human knowledge and the knowledge of other animals, that is, if there is a reason to think that they are different in kind, then that reason must be found elsewhere.

4

Human Knowledge and Reflection

HUMAN beings sometimes reflect on their beliefs. We sometimes wonder whether the beliefs we have are ones we ought to have. And we sometimes wonder, about beliefs we might come to adopt, whether we ought to adopt them. More than this, such reflection does not seem, at least typically, to be an idle academic exercise. Rather, we reflect on our beliefs because we wish to take an active role in shaping the beliefs we come to have and revising the beliefs we already accept. When we notice that a belief we already accept seems unjustified, this, by itself, at least typically, is sufficient to cause us to give up the belief. And when we notice that a belief we might come to accept is one that is fully justified for us, this too, by itself, is typically sufficient to bring about a change in our beliefs. Reflection seems to guide belief acquisition, retention, and revision. It is, it seems, an important part of human cognition.

Reflection is also something that seems to distinguish human cognition from the cognition of other animals. While non-human animals, as I have argued, may certainly be credited with beliefs, and their beliefs may be responsive to features of the environment in important ways, non-human animals do not reflect on the character of their beliefs and the logical relations among them. Dogs may certainly come to believe that a squirrel has run up a particular tree, but there is no reason whatsoever to think that dogs ever stop to consider whether they are fully justified in believing that a squirrel has run up a particular tree. They do not stop to consider whether their beliefs about the squirrel stand in the right logical relations to their evidence. And they do not self-consciously consider the merits of various alternative explanations of a body of data, settling on a particular explanation only after its superior epistemic credentials have been adequately demonstrated.

These kinds of considerations have led some philosophers to suggest that the cognitive states of non-human animals are not fully deserving of the title 'knowledge', or, at a minimum, if they are to be called knowledge at all, they are a sort of low-grade knowledge, different in kind, and inferior to, the kind of knowledge human beings are capable of and to which we ought to aspire. Genuine knowledge requires a certain degree of self-conscious reflection, and this is something that only human beings may attain.

Thus, as mentioned earlier, Ernest Sosa draws a distinction between 'animal knowledge' and 'reflective knowledge':

> One has *animal knowledge* about one's environment, one's past, and one's own experience if one's judgments and beliefs about these are direct responses to their impact—e.g., through perception or memory—with little or no benefit of reflection or understanding. One has *reflective knowledge* if one's judgment or belief manifests not only such direct response to the fact known but also understanding of its place in a wider whole that includes one's belief and knowledge of it and how these come about.[1]

Sosa comments that 'reflective knowledge is better justified than corresponding animal knowledge',[2] and, although one might think that human beings have both kinds of knowledge, Sosa goes on to

---

[1] Ernest Sosa, 'Knowledge and Intellectual Virtue', in *Knowledge in Perspective: Selected Essays in Epistemology* (Cambridge University Press, 1991), 240.
[2] Ibid. 240.

claim that 'no human being blessed with reason has merely animal knowledge of the sort attainable by beasts', for a 'reason-endowed being automatically monitors[3] his background information and his sensory input for contrary evidence and automatically opts for the most coherent hypothesis even when he responds most directly to sensory stimuli'.[4] What initially may have seemed like a distinction between two kinds of knowledge of which humans are capable, one that we share with other animals and one that is uniquely our own, turns out on closer examination to be a distinction between all human knowledge on the one hand, and all non-human animal knowledge on the other.

Many epistemologists who have not written about differences between human and non-human animal knowledge, but have merely sought to explain what knowledge consists in, have offered accounts that make self-conscious reflection an essential ingredient of knowledge. Laurence BonJour, in his book, *The Structure of Empirical Knowledge*,[5] defended a coherence theory of justification. On BonJour's view, knowledge requires justified belief, and an individual's belief is only justified if it coheres with the other beliefs that individual holds. But as BonJour argues, it is not sufficient for justification that a belief as a matter of fact cohere with other beliefs held; rather, on BonJour's view, a belief must be held precisely in virtue of the recognition of its coherence with other beliefs. What

---

[3] Talk of 'automatically monitoring' here is problematic. If all this comes to is showing some responsiveness to contrary evidence, then many non-human animals surely meet this condition, contrary to Sosa's explicitly stated intentions; indeed, such responsiveness is arguably a necessary condition for having beliefs at all. (Sosa cannot lay too much stress on the requirement of opting for the 'most coherent hypothesis' without the consequence that even human beings fail to satisfy the condition.) Non-human animals are genuinely ruled out of the category of reflective knowledge, it seems, only if talk of an agent monitoring beliefs, however automatically, requires some degree of self-conscious scrutiny, or at least some beliefs about one's own beliefs. This reading seems to fit better with talk of the specifically human knowledge as 'reflective', as well as the requirement that there be 'understanding of [a belief's] place in a wider whole that includes one's belief and knowledge of it and how these came about'.   [4] Ibid. 240.

[5] (Harvard University Press, 1985).

this requires, as BonJour makes plain, is that one should reflect on the content of one's beliefs and the logical relations among them. Without such reflection, knowledge is impossible.

BonJour's insistence on a reflective understanding of the epistemic credentials of one's beliefs is, of course, unrelated to his defense of coherentism in that book. Rather, it is a product of BonJour's commitment to internalism about justification, and such internalism may just as easily be combined with foundationalism. Indeed, BonJour himself has since rejected coherentism, and his new view combines the old commitment to internalism with an explicitly foundationalist account of justification.[6] Here too then, knowledge is seen as requiring a certain kind of reflection, reflection on the epistemic credentials of one's belief. And, of course, if this is required for knowledge, then human beings may have it, but non-human animals may not.

In this chapter I examine the view that human knowledge requires some sort of self-conscious reflection on one's beliefs and the relations among them. Such a requirement on human knowledge would make it different in kind from the knowledge of non-human animals. But while it is true that humans are capable of intellectual activities which other animals are not, I argue here that human knowledge and the knowledge of non-human animals is not different in kind, and that human knowledge requires no sort of reflection at all.

4.1 Reflection in Descartes

The idea that reflection is an essential ingredient for knowledge is not, of course, new. It was the centerpiece of Descartes's epistemology, and because the role of reflection is so clear there, I want to

---

[6] Laurence BonJour, 'The Dialectic of Foundationalism and Coherentism', in J. Greco and E. Sosa (eds.), *The Blackwell Guide to Epistemology* (Blackwell, 1999), 117–42, and 'Toward a Defense of Empirical Foundationalism', in Michael DePaul (ed.), *Resurrecting Old-Fashioned Foundationalism* (Rowman & Littlefield, 2001), 21–38.

begin with a brief discussion of the work that reflection does for Descartes.

Reflection plays two distinct roles in leading an agent to improve his epistemic situation, according to Descartes. First, reflection is called upon to reveal the defects of the unreflective agent's position. Second, reflection is called upon to remedy those defects. Let's examine each of these roles.

In *Meditation I*, Descartes reveals that his current epistemic situation is defective. He realizes that he has had many false beliefs in the past, and that many of his current beliefs, being arrived at on the basis of past beliefs, are thus likely to be false as well. All of this is revealed by way of introspection or reflection. Moreover, once Descartes introduces the method of doubt, that he will suspend belief in everything about which it is possible to be mistaken, nothing more than introspection is required to see that everything can be doubted. Descartes accordingly resolves to suspend all belief, and that he has succeeded in doing this can be determined by introspection as well. The negative part of Descartes's program, described in *Meditation I*, is carried out under the aegis of the faculty of introspection.

Likewise, the positive part of Descartes's program is supervised by introspection. On Descartes's view, belief is now to be achieved by acts of will, which are clearly introspectable, and these acts of will are to be exerted in virtue of the recognition of the clarity and distinctness of certain ideas. The entire process of belief acquisition is thus certified by the faculty of introspection.

Descartes's theory of justification is a historical theory: he believes that the justificatory status of a belief is dependent upon its ancestry. Only those beliefs that are arrived at in the appropriate way are to count as justified. By choosing our beliefs on the basis of the appropriate introspectable features of our minds, we may certify, by introspection, that our beliefs do indeed meet the appropriate standards.

Introspection is thus called upon to reveal the defects of our current epistemic situation, to provide the will with the appropriate materials with which to remedy the situation, and to certify that those defects have been remedied.

Whatever other defects this procedure may have, and it has a great many, there is one practical difficulty it faces. It is obvious that this procedure is very slow. Any agent who seeks to arrive at all of his beliefs in this way will have very few beliefs. There can be little doubt that Descartes was interested in giving epistemic advice that was practical, and so someone who was otherwise completely untroubled by Descartes's description of the proper way to acquire beliefs would at least have to concern himself with this practical difficulty. Let me suggest some short cuts, then, for what I will call the Impatient Cartesian. I will not suggest that Descartes would have endorsed these short cuts, but I argue below that many contemporary epistemologists would.

Consider the negative part of Descartes's program: rejecting all those beliefs about which it is possible to be wrong. Descartes is aware that this is not easy. There are habits of belief acquisition that are deeply ingrained in us and that are very hard to overcome. If one were to take Descartes seriously in his suggestion that we must begin by giving up all these habits of belief acquisition, we might never get to the positive part of Descartes's program. It may not, however, be necessary to overcome all these habits, for if prior to ridding ourselves of our habits of belief acquisition, we simply determine which of them are defective, we might be able to spend our time better. Many of our current unreflective belief-acquisition procedures may, after all, turn out to be adequate as they stand. Those that are adequate may be left in place with no harm done; those that are not will have to be weeded out. This will save us the time involved in first giving up certain habits and then, perhaps, attempting to acquire those very same habits again.

My Impatient Cartesian will think that all this can be accomplished by way of introspection, just as Descartes allowed his project to be supervised under the aegis of introspection. One might even attempt to enlist Descartes's support. Descartes did, after all, claim that 'I can affirm with certainty that there is nothing in me of which I am not in any way conscious'.[7] If the mind is, in this way, wholly transparent to introspection, my program for the Impatient Cartesian should be one that Descartes himself would endorse. On this account, the method of doubt is nothing more than a literary device for making vivid the possibility of error.

4.2 Internalism and the Impatient Cartesian

Current internalists about justification are Impatient Cartesians. It is, of course, impossible to survey all contemporary internalists, so I will examine two representative figures, Roderick Chisholm and the Laurence BonJour of *The Structure of Empirical Knowledge*. In each case, I will examine the extent to which introspection is implicated in the epistemic advice they offer concerned agents. I will argue that introspection plays a central role.

According to Chisholm, if we wish to know whether a particular belief is justified, we must engage in Socratic questioning. If I want to know whether my belief that *p* is justified, I must ask myself, 'What justification do I have for counting this as something that is evident?' or 'What justification do I have for thinking that this is true?'[8] I am thus to ask myself what my reasons are for holding the belief, and I am to answer this question by introspecting. Similarly, when I find that my reason for believing that *p* is that *q*, I am to ask myself the same question about my belief that *q*. I am to continue this process until I reach some proposition that is directly evident. That a proposition is directly evident is recognizable through introspection.

Chisholm proceeds to elaborate on the connection that must obtain between directly evident propositions and those that are only

[7] *The Philosophical Works of Descartes*, ed. E. S. Haldane and G. R. T. Ross (Cambridge University Press, 1931), ii. 13.

[8] Roderick Chisholm, *Theory of Knowledge*, 2nd edn. (Prentice-Hall, 1977), 17.

indirectly evident if the latter are to be justified at all. That these conditions obtain can be recognized by introspection.[9]

Thus, unlike Descartes, Chisholm does not require that we begin the epistemological project by rejecting all our beliefs. Instead, we may examine the beliefs we currently have and see whether they meet the appropriate standards. Only those that fail to meet these standards need to be rejected. All this is accomplished by means of introspection. In short, Chisholm adopts the program of the Impatient Cartesian.

Similarly, consider Laurence BonJour's coherentist account of justification.[10] According to BonJour, a belief is justified for an agent only if it coheres with the rest of that agent's beliefs. BonJour is at great pains to argue that both an agent's beliefs and the coherence relation itself are available to introspection.[11]

It would be possible, of course, to adopt an externalist version of coherentism. Such a view would hold that the person whose belief is justified need himself have no cognitive access to the fact of coherence, that his belief is justified whether or not such coherence is cognitively accessible to him (or, presumably, to anyone). But such a view is unacceptable . . .[12]

As BonJour makes abundantly clear, the question about cognitive accessibility is a question about the faculty of introspection.[13]

BonJour is thus offering the truth-seeking agent a certain bit of epistemic advice. We are to introspect and determine whether our beliefs cohere; those that do not are to be rejected, and those that do cohere are to be retained. Although BonJour does not believe that the faculty of introspection is infallible, he does, like Descartes, call on this faculty to locate our cognitive errors, to provide the materials for correcting those errors, and to certify that the correction has taken place. BonJour too adopts the program of the Impatient Cartesian.

[9] Roderick Chisholm, *Theory of Knowledge*, 2nd edn. (Prentice-Hall, 1977), 62–86.
[10] *The Structure of Empirical Knowledge*.   [11] Ibid. esp. 101–6.
[12] Ibid. 101.   [13] Ibid. 137–8.

I cannot examine all current foundationalist and coherentist views here. I do believe, however, that Chisholm and BonJour are not idiosyncratic in this respect: current internalist foundationalists and coherentists are all Impatient Cartesians. All these philosophers are committed to embarking on the project of epistemic self-improvement in a way that gives introspection a very central role. It is thus well worth asking whether introspection is well suited to play this role. If we allow introspection to play the role that these philosophers advise, what will the likely results be?

4.3 Real introspection

Let me begin with an account of a study conducted by Nisbett and Wilson.

passers-by in a shopping mall were invited to examine an array of consumer goods (four nightgowns in one study, four identical nylon pantyhose in another) and to rate their quality. There was a pronounced position effect on the evaluations, such that the right-most garments were heavily preferred to the left-most garments. When questioned about the effect of the garments' position on their choices, virtually all subjects denied such an influence (usually with a tone of annoyance or of concern for the experimenter's sanity).[14]

This is an interesting case to begin with because the position effect presents a strong prima-facie case of faulty inference. In evaluating various consumer goods, we should not be influenced by their relative position; nevertheless, it seems that we are. Subjects in this study, however, are unaware that their judgments are affected by the relative position of the goods being evaluated. Moreover, it seems quite clear that asking these subjects to introspect more carefully —'Are you sure you weren't influenced by the fact that the garment you chose was on the right?'—would not make them better

---

[14] Richard Nisbett and Lee Ross, *Human Inference: Strategies and Shortcomings of Social Judgment* (Prentice-Hall, 1980), 207.

acquainted with the source of their judgments. Here then is a case in which we might hope that the concerned truth-seeker would notice his faulty pattern of inference and come to reject it; but introspection is no help here. On introspecting, subjects believe that they are evaluating these goods in just the way they ought to. Unreflective agents are thus influenced by the position effect. Agents who are asked to introspect to determine the reliability of the process by which their judgment is reached will not notice that they are so influenced, and will thus conclude that they have reasoned correctly. Far from helping in the process of self-correction, introspection here merely results in a more confident, though no less misguided, agent. One should not think that an unusually responsible or circumspect agent would be affected differently here. Especially responsible agents may be more willing than most to recognize their own mistakes when they are pointed out. There is no reason, however, to think that responsible agents are any less susceptible to this illusion.

Consider, in particular, how agents in the situation described would proceed if they were to follow the advice offered by Chisholm or by BonJour. Chisholm suggests that agents ask themselves why it is reasonable to think some particular belief to be true. In order to answer this question, they are instructed to introspect. Now consider the agent who believes, in the situation described, that the nightgown on the right is the best. He is supposed to ask himself what reason he has for thinking this true. What the experiment tells us is that he will take himself to have objectively good reasons for his belief; he will take himself to have noticed features of the nightgown on the right that make it the best of the lot. Now I do not pretend to have a Chisholmian deduction from directly evident propositions here, but if the Chisholmian system can ever show evaluative propositions to be justified, it will show this proposition to be justified. The agent here will take himself to have just the kind of evidence he has in the standard case. Chisholm's advice will thus lead him to the conclusion that he is justified in this case, and that he should therefore continue to hold his belief.

BonJour's advice does no better. The agent, according to BonJour, should ask himself whether his belief that the night-gown on the right is best coheres with the rest of his beliefs. Now I'm not at all sure how an agent is supposed to go about answering this question, but this much is clear: the case for coherence in this instance is as good as it ever gets in evaluative judgments. When the agent checks to see how well this belief coheres with the rest of his beliefs, he will find that it passes the test; he should thus continue to hold the belief.

Thus, in both the case of the advice offered by Chisholm and that offered by BonJour, we find that agents who arrive at their beliefs as a result of the position effect will come to believe, after taking the proffered advice, that they are in fact justified in their beliefs. Introspection here is powerless to detect the error made, and when called into service as a source of epistemic improvement it merely serves to certify a misguided process of belief acquisition. Agents who do not seek out the advice of Chisholm and BonJour will arrive at their beliefs in an unreflective and mistaken fashion: those who do seek out their advice will continue to err, but will add to their stock of beliefs the belief that they are fully justified in their judgments.

This case is not unusual or atypical. Consider Tversky and Kahneman's work on the anchoring effect.[15] Subjects were asked the percentage of African members of the United Nations. A roulette wheel was spun, and subjects were asked whether the number that turned up was too high or too low. In those cases where the roulette wheel provided an anchor of 10, the mean estimate was 25; where the anchor was 65, the mean estimate was 45. It is quite clear that subjects were influenced in their judgment by the result of the spin of the roulette wheel. None of the subjects, however, showed any awareness of this influence; nor is there reason to think that asking

[15] Amos Tversky and Daniel Kahneman, 'Judgment under Uncertainty: Heuristics and Biases', repr. in D. Kahneman, P. Slovic, and A. Tversky (eds.), *Judgment under Uncertainty: Heuristics and Biases* (Cambridge University Press, 1982), 14.

the subject to introspect more carefully here would provide much assistance. Once again, the suggestion that introspection may provide us with a valuable check on the reliability of our inference is shown to fail. It is clear that the advice that foundationalists and coherentists offer here would only add the mistake of further confidence to an already misguided agent.

Both of the cases thus far described involve subjects' failures to detect factors influencing their judgments. These are not, however, the only kind of errors subjects make in attempting to discover the source of their judgments by introspection. Factors that influence our judgments may be overlooked, but, in addition, factors we believe to influence our judgments may have little or no influence on us. Nisbett and Ross had subjects read a passage describing a baby's accidental drowning; subjects were then asked to pick out those portions of the passage that they thought were most responsible for its emotional impact. The portions that were indicated by the subjects were just the ones that Nisbett and Ross themselves thought were most responsible for its dramatic effect. When the same passage was given to a different group of subjects with the indicated passages removed, however, they rated it as having the very same emotional impact as the first group.[16] Subjects in the first group, as well as Nisbett and Ross themselves, thus believed that the source of their emotional reaction could be traced to certain portions of the passage, but they were mistaken. Introspection simply does not provide us with accurate information about the etiology of our mental states. This kind of mistake is especially important to the Chisholmian program, for there introspection is supposed to inform the agent as to his reasons for belief. The information introspection gives in this case is mistaken. Even in the coherentist case, however, the mistaken belief about the source of one's judgment will have a deleterious effect, for it will help to smooth the coherence relations of the belief in question with the

[16] Nisbett and Ross, *Human Inference*, 209.

remainder of one's body of beliefs. Here too then introspection adds nothing more than misguided confidence to the errors that are already being made.

Mistakes of this sort also occur in perceptual cases. Passengers on a plane are able to tell when the plane is headed up or down, right or left. This is something, it seems, that one detects visually. The orientation of the plane, however, is not detected by visual means at all, as is revealed by noticing that the very same effect occurs even on night flights when there is no possible visual source of information about the plane's orientation. Information about the orientation of the plane is conveyed not visually, but kinesthetically: one detects the orientation of the plane by detecting the orientation of one's body. Careful introspection is powerless to detect the source of information. The illusion that the orientation of the plane is detected visually persists even when one knows that it is detected kinesthetically.

There is, then, an important range of cases in which introspection systematically misleads subjects about the sources of their beliefs. Subjects who undertake the project of epistemic self-evaluation by attempting to introspect the source of their beliefs will, at least in the kinds of cases described, misdiagnose their reasons for belief. The project of self-evaluation and self-correction thus gets off on the wrong foot. In some cases, such as the mistaken belief about the source of information about an airplane's orientation, the mistake is harmless. In this case, subjects mistakenly believe that their information is obtained visually, but they are not mistaken in their belief that they can reliably detect the orientation of the plane. In other cases, however, the mistake is more significant. Processes that are in fact unreliable are not recognized as such. Factors that should not influence a subject's judgment are not recognized as influential. In cases such as these, introspection is not only powerless to detect the errors that we make, but in misdiagnosing the source of our judgments and our reasons for believing, the reliance on introspection as a tool for self-evaluation merely instills a false sense of confidence in an already misguided agent.

4.4 Doesn't this just show that introspection is fallible?

It may be objected that the cases I have described thus far show nothing more than that introspection is not infallible. Once one acknowledges that introspection is not infallible, one will expect that there should be cases, like those described, in which introspective reports on the nature of one's mental processes will be mistaken. It is one thing to claim that introspection is fallible; quite another, however, to claim that introspection is unreliable.

I wish to argue that the cases described, and others like them, support the stronger thesis that introspective reports of mental processes are unreliable for the purposes intended here. The cases thus far described are not ones where there is interference with an otherwise reliable process; nor are these cases where circumstances are created in the psychological laboratory that are unlike those encountered in the ordinary course of events. Rather, the cases described are ones where introspection is allowed to work as it would in ordinary circumstances, and yet the typical result is a mistaken belief about the agent's process of belief acquisition or retention. For an agent to be mistaken about such a process is to be mistaken about his reason for belief. These cases shift the burden of proof onto those who would defend introspection as the touchstone of epistemic advice.

Indeed, I wish to argue that the situation is even worse than this. Introspection is not merely unreliable for these purposes; it does not merely fail to give us accurate information about our reasons for belief. A tendency to rely on introspection in pursuing the project of epistemic self-improvement will most likely lull the agent into a false sense of security. Introspecting in order to check on the justificatory status of one's processes of belief acquisition will likely lead to the belief that these processes are justified, regardless of their reliability. In order to see why this is so, we need to look at studies on features of belief acquisition in general.

In studies of hypothesis testing in a variety of situations, two kinds of confirmation bias have been detected. First, subjects seeking to test a hypothesis tend to seek out confirming instances and do not attempt to check for disconfirming information. Second, when disconfirming information is nevertheless encountered, it tends to be taken far less seriously than confirming information, even when the hypothesis being tested was not antecedently believed.

Peter Wason[17] gave subjects a sequence of three numbers and told them that the sequence conformed to some general rule. Subjects were asked to try to discover this rule by proposing three number sequences that, they would be told, either conformed or failed to conform to the rule. Subjects were asked to explain, as they proposed each sequence, what it was they were doing. Typical subjects had a hypothesis in mind that they were testing, but tested the hypothesis by examining only confirming instances of it. When a number of confirming instances were piled up, they would announce that they had discovered the rule governing the initial sequence. Strangely, when subjects were told that they had not discovered the rule, in more than half the cases the next sequence tested was an instance of the very rule they had just been told was incorrect.

Lord, Ross, and Lepper[18] studied confirmation bias in a somewhat more naturalistic setting. Subjects were recruited in two groups; one group believed that capital punishment has deterrent effects, while the other group believed that it does not. Each group read summaries of two studies, one of which supported the claim that capital punishment has deterrent effects, the other supporting

[17] Peter Wason, 'On the Failure to Eliminate Hypotheses in a Conceptual Task', *Quarterly Journal of Experimental Psychology*, 12 (1960), 129–40; also reported in Peter Wason and Philip Johnson-Laird, *Psychology of Reasoning: Structure and Content* (Harvard University Press, 1972), 204–14.

[18] C. Lord, L. Ross, and M. Lepper, 'Biased Assimilation and Attitude Polarization: The Effects of Prior Theories on Subsequently Considered Evidence', *Journal of Personality and Social Psychology*, 34 (1979); also reported in Nisbett and Ross, *Human Inference*, 170–2.

the claim that it does not. The methods of the studies varied. One study compared a given state at different times, with and without capital punishment. The other study compared different states, with and without capital punishment, at the same times.

Subjects found the studies that supported their previously held views to be well conducted and convincing, while those supporting the contrary view were found to have significant methodological flaws. Those subjects who read a study that ran contrary to their own view first were not significantly affected by it. Those who read a study that supported their opinion first were even more convinced that they were correct. After both groups read one study supporting each view, each group was more strongly convinced that the view they held before walking in to the experiment was correct.

Nisbett and Ross comment,

> Before the advent of modern social science, many questions, like the issue of the deterrent value of capital punishment, were ones for which there really was no empirical evidence one way or the other . . . One might expect, though, that once genuine empirical evidence for such questions became available, that evidence would sway opinion to whichever side it supported or, if the evidence were mixed, that it would serve to moderate opposing views. Instead, the effect of introducing mixed evidence may be to *polarize* public opinion . . . [19]

The existence of confirmation bias provides a global reason for thinking that responsible agents are unlikely to discover, at least by way of introspection, the extent of their epistemic shortcomings. Most agents think of themselves as tolerably reliable in their acquisition of belief, and with good reason. Once this belief is in place, however, our natural confirmation bias will serve to insulate it from disconfirming evidence. Especially in the case of an agent's belief in his own reliability, this discounting of disconfirming evidence will not seem at all strained. Everyone, after all, makes mistakes; that an

---

[19] Nisbett and Ross, *Human Inference*, 171.

agent discovers he has made a mistake on a particular occasion should not, it seems, lead to general doubts about the reliability of his inferences. Precisely because this is so, one's mistakes will not, ordinarily, take on any special salience; because they are not especially salient, they will not be remembered as well.[20] Thus, when an agent becomes unusually reflective and tries to survey his past performance, the performance he is able to remember further confirms his earlier assessment of his own reliability. Our natural confirmation bias thus not only hides its own working from us; it serves to make our inferential shortcomings in general more difficult to detect. Thus, those who introspect in order to check on the reliability of their processes of belief acquisition are liable to find that they pass the test with flying colors.

Some will object that I have been conflating questions about justification with questions about the reliability of processes of belief-acquisition. Chisholm and BonJour attempt to give agents advice that will result in justified beliefs. Neither of them, however, equate justified belief with reliably produced belief. All I have shown, it will be argued, is that following their advice will fail to improve reliability. I have not shown, however, that following their advice will fail to lead to justified belief.

It is possible to divorce one's concept of justification from reliability in this way. I certainly do not wish to presuppose a reliabilist account of justification here. On the other hand, the proposed defense of Chisholm and BonJour is not without its cost. If one does so divorce one's concept of justification from that of reliability, it becomes very hard to say why one should care to have justified beliefs. I began this chapter by assuming that the truth-seeking agent is looking for advice to improve his epistemic performance, and that Chisholm and BonJour mean to offer this agent just such advice. If we now say that following their advice will lead to justified belief, but assuring that one's beliefs are justified will not aid in

[20] See e.g. ibid. 180–3.

getting at the truth, then the project of achieving justified beliefs seems pointless.

Like Descartes, I assume that the responsible epistemic agent is truth-seeking and that in attempting to improve his epistemic situation he is attempting to improve his reliability; he wishes to be more effective in getting at the truth. If Chisholm and BonJour respond to the examples I have cited by allowing that justification does not help in getting at the truth, then they have conceded my point.

4.5 Introspection and epistemic self-improvement

Descartes held that the mind is wholly transparent to introspection. Such a view of the mind is obviously incompatible with the data. Most importantly, those features of our beliefs in virtue of which they are either justified or unjustified are not transparent to introspection, so long as we are working with a concept of justification that is worth caring about. In light of the currently available data, what view should we have of the powers and workings of introspection?

The first point to make is that our processes of belief acquisition, and indeed mental processes in general, are largely unavailable to introspection. Were this not so, cognitive psychology would be easy; but it is not easy. It has been known for quite some time that the factors that influence our perceptual beliefs are ones of which we are largely unaware through introspection. Now that a good deal of data on inference have begun to become available, it seems that, in the case of inference just as much as perception, introspection reveals very little about the nature of our mental processes.

Our introspective reports on mental processes involve a good deal of rational reconstruction, as Daniel Dennett has suggested.[21] Moreover, as the experimental data reveal, this rational reconstruction involves heavy reliance on the presupposition of our own

[21] Daniel Dennett, *Brainstorms* (Bradford Books, 1978), 88.

reliability. In attempting to figure out what process is responsible for one of our beliefs, we typically begin by assuming our own rationality[22] and then try to figure out what a rational person would have done. This is not to say, of course, that this process of rational reconstruction occurs consciously. Nevertheless, we must posit such inferences to make sense of the experimental data. How else could we possibly explain that those who are influenced by the position effect in judging the quality of consumer goods explain the source of their judgments as lying in objective features of the goods whose quality they judge?

It is for precisely this reason that introspection is so ill-suited to the task of providing agents with epistemic advice. Even if one thought that this process of rational reconstruction involving heavy reliance on the assumption of rationality were reliable, perhaps because we are, after all, quite reliable in our processes of belief acquisition, one would still be forced to the conclusion that introspection is badly suited for the project of epistemic self-improvement. What is needed for the epistemic project to work is the ability to recognize our epistemic shortcomings. But whatever success we have in recognizing our processes of belief acquisition is due to our reliance on the assumption of rationality, and it is precisely our reliance on this assumption that makes it difficult for us to recognize our mistakes. Here, as elsewhere, our epistemic successes and failures are to be explained as products of one and the same underlying process. In this case, however, the pattern of our failures is of profound epistemic importance. It blinds us to exactly those areas in which our performance most needs improvement.

I have argued that introspection is ill-suited to play the central role in epistemic self-improvement that it has been widely thought

---

[22] Some may argue that the assumption of rationality is indispensable, for without such an assumption we cannot even think of ourselves as believers. Although it is certainly true that some degree of rationality is required if a subject is to have beliefs at all, the above examples make abundantly clear that far less rationality is required for belief attribution than is actually assumed by agents in reconstructing their own inference patterns.

to play at least since Descartes. This is not because I believe the project of self-improvement to be pointless, but rather because I believe that project to require a more subtle understanding than mere introspection can provide. The moral of my story is obvious. The very important project of epistemic self-improvement can only succeed with the help of cognitive psychology. We should accept no substitutes.

4.6 Idealized reflection: Coherence theories

The kind of reflection that typically goes on in real human agents is thus not the sort of thing that we would want to encourage. It does not improve one's epistemic situation; it does not typically aid in the project of getting an accurate understanding of the world; in cases where epistemic improvement is needed, it typically results in a more confident, but no less misguided, epistemic agent. It would clearly be unreasonable to suggest that this sort of process is an essential ingredient in knowledge.

But those who defend some kind of reflection requirement will insist that the entire discussion thus far has no bearing on their views. Those who favor reflection as a requirement for knowledge do not merely endorse the actually existing practice of reflection, nor do they propose certain standards for reflection and then suggest that agents should try to meet them. Rather, certain standards for reflection are proposed, and knowledge is said to require actually meeting these standards. If agents who try to meet the standards frequently fail, it will be said, this hardly shows that the proposed standards are not good ones; and it certainly does not show that the proposed standards need not be met if genuine knowledge is to be achieved.

I do not believe that what actually happens when agents try to meet a set of standards is as irrelevant to the evaluation of those standards as this response would suggest. But I do not want to argue this point. It is clear that having agents try to meet the standards of reflection that epistemologists have proposed would not have a beneficial effect on epistemic practice. But would it be reasonable, none the less, to insist that actually meeting these standards is required if knowledge is to be attained? We will consider two kinds of reflective standards that have been proposed: in this section we will examine coherentist requirements on reflection; in the next, we will examine foundationalist requirements.

So let us return, once again, to Laurence BonJour's version of the coherence theory, which requires a substantial amount of reflection on the character of, and relations among, one's beliefs. BonJour writes,

According to a coherence theory of empirical justification, as so far charac-terized, the epistemic justification of an empirical belief derives entirely from its coherence with the believer's overall system of empirical beliefs and not at all from any sort of factor outside that system. What we must now ask is whether and how the fact that a belief coheres in this way is cognitively accessible to the believer himself, so that it can give him a reason for accepting the belief.[23]

What makes BonJour an internalist about justification is this claim that the coherence of one belief with others is 'cognitively access-ible' to an agent, and that it is for this reason that coherence may provide an agent with justification. To say that coherence is cognit-ively accessible to an agent is just to say that it is available on reflection, and the knowing agent must be reflectively aware of the coherence of his beliefs. The requirement of cognitive accessibility, however, is not an easy one to meet. As BonJour notes, 'if the fact of coherence is to be accessible to the believer, it follows that he must somehow have an adequate grasp of his total system of beliefs, since it is coherence with this system which is at issue'.[24] But to what extent is one's total system of beliefs actually available to an agent on reflection?

[23] BonJour, *The Structure of Empirical Knowledge*, 101.   [24] Ibid. 102.

Note how important this issue is. If I am considering whether a particular belief of mine is justified, and I reflect on the contents of my other beliefs, I simply will not meet BonJour's standard if reflection reveals to me only a proper subset of my beliefs. A given belief may be coherent with a proper subset of one's beliefs, and yet fail to cohere with one's total system; such a belief would then be unjustified. So reflecting on one's beliefs, and, in practice, merely coming to grips with only a proper subset of them, will not put one in a position to even address the question of coherence that BonJour insists we address. Somehow, we must grasp our entire system of beliefs.

Now I think it is safe to say that no human being ever does this, and, indeed, no human being is even capable of it. While I have frequently reflected on my beliefs and self-consciously raised questions about their coherence, the number of beliefs I am capable of entertaining at any given time is quite small in comparison with the total body of my beliefs. And in this respect, I do not compare unfavorably with other human beings. Grasping one's total body of beliefs is something that simply cannot be done. And if it is nevertheless insisted that it is a requirement for knowledge, then knowledge is something that no one ever has. The requirement of reflection would thus not distinguish human beings from other animals. Knowledge simply does not exist on this view.

Grasping one's entire corpus of beliefs is only the beginning of BonJour's problem. For even if one could grasp all one's beliefs, one would still need to assess their coherence, and whether they are coherent would have to be something available to a knowing agent upon reflection. Now one necessary condition for the coherence of a body of beliefs is that they be consistent.[25] To what extent, then, is the consistency of a body of beliefs accessible to an agent? Consider, for example, the axioms of Frege's *Basic Laws of Arithmetic*. Frege thought long and hard about these axioms. After extraordinarily

<hr>

[25] BonJour, *The Structure of Empirical Knowledge*, 95.

careful consideration, he adopted them as the foundation of his system. He clearly believed each of the axioms to be true and, of course, he believed them to be jointly consistent. Frege was, famously, mistaken. As Russell demonstrated in a letter to Frege, the axioms of the *Basic Laws* were inconsistent.

Now it is clear that Frege was not simply being careless. We are not considering an agent who arrived at his beliefs in a haphazard way, or even the case of an agent who carefully arrived at each of his beliefs individually, but never considered the question of their consistency. I think it is safe to say that Frege arrived at his beliefs in the axioms of the *Basic Laws* as carefully and self-consciously as an agent can. Nevertheless, the fact of their inconsistency eluded him.

According to BonJour, the coherence or incoherence of a set of beliefs is cognitively accessible to an agent. Since coherence requires consistency, the consistency of a set of beliefs must also be cognitively accessible to an agent. Thus, according to BonJour, the inconsistency of the axioms of the *Basic Laws* was actually cognitively accessible to Frege from the very beginning. What does BonJour mean by this claim of cognitive accessibility? What reason, if any, is there to think that BonJour is correct?

Before addressing these two questions, I want to introduce two more examples, each of which demonstrates the difficulty of determining whether a set of beliefs is actually coherent. Although BonJour is certainly not committed to the claim that coherence is easy to determine, I do not believe that the difficulty of determining coherence is entirely irrelevant either.

In a famous criticism of the coherence theory, Moritz Schlick[26] claimed that fairy tales and novels satisfy coherentist requirements for justified belief. Although I do not wish to endorse Schlick's criticism, I do wish to appropriate one of his examples. Let us consider the case of a short novel, and let us ask whether the sentences of the

---

[26] Moritz Schlick, 'The Foundation of Knowledge', in A. J. Ayer (ed.), *Logical Positivism* (Free Press, 1959), 215.

novel satisfy BonJour's requirement of coherence. First, of course, the novel must not be internally inconsistent. As the Frege example should alert us, determining consistency is no easy task. Frege was working with a small number of axioms. Even a short novel of 200 pages is likely to contain somewhere in the neighborhood of 5,000 sentences. If the inconsistency of the *Basic Laws* could elude Frege, it does not tax the imagination to suppose that inconsistency could arise in a short novel without coming to the attention of even the most careful reader. Now consider how many times this problem is magnified when we move from the 5,000 sentences of a short novel to the corpus of an adult's beliefs. The problem of hidden inconsistency is highly non-trivial.

Finally, let us consider cases involving inference to the best explanation. BonJour believes that the coherence of a body of beliefs has a great deal to do with the explanatory relations among them.[27] Cases involving inference to the best explanation may involve huge bodies of data and theory directly; of course, on any coherentist account, such inference will indirectly involve all an agent's beliefs. In actual practice, there is typically a social dimension to inference to the best explanation: potential explanations are proposed to colleagues and tested against their reactions. The mechanism of publication assures that potential explanations are widely aired. On BonJour's account, however, the coherence of a set of beliefs is supposed to be 'internally available' and 'cognitively accessible' to an agent. Introspection alone should suffice, on BonJour's account, for determining the best explanation of a set of beliefs. There can be little doubt that inference to the best explanation can be astoundingly difficult. BonJour seems to endow the faculty of introspection with remarkable abilities.

Given how difficult coherence is to determine, and given how easily even careful and insightful agents can go wrong about coherence, what could BonJour mean in claiming that coherence is

---

[27] BonJour, *The Structure of Empirical Knowledge*, 98.

cognitively accessible to an agent? One clue to answering this question can be found in BonJour's criticism of reliabilism as a theory of justification. Reliabilists hold that a belief is justified just in case it is produced by a reliable process.[28] BonJour describes a number of cases[29] in which a belief is in fact reliably produced, and yet, intuitively, we would say that the agent has excellent reason to reject his belief. BonJour concludes that although the belief is clearly unjustified, reliabilists are committed to claiming that the belief is justified. Reliabilism is thus shown to be mistaken as a theory of justification. BonJour's explanation of the reliabilist's error, however, is extremely revealing.

these cases and the modifications made in response to them also suggest an important moral which leads to a basic intuitive objection to externalism: external or objective reliability is not enough to offset subjective irrationality. If the acceptance of a belief is seriously unreasonable or unwarranted from the believer's own standpoint, then the mere fact that unbeknownst to him its existence in those circumstances lawfully guarantees its truth will not suffice to render the belief epistemically justified . . .[30]

Justification may not be explained in terms of objective reliability because a belief may be reliably produced and yet 'seriously unreasonable or unwarranted from the believer's own standpoint'. Reliability is thus too distant from the agent's point of view. It is not cognitively accessible to the agent.

But how is coherence supposed to differ from reliability in this regard? Is it impossible for the objective facts about coherence to differ from their appearance 'from the believer's own standpoint'? Even if we choose a believer as careful and insightful as Frege, there may be substantial gaps between the appearance and the reality of coherence. Coherence may be just as external to an agent's point of view as reliability. The very argument that BonJour uses against

[28] See A. Goldman, 'What is Justified Belief?,' in *Liaisons: Philosophy Meets the Cognitive and Social Sciences* (MIT Press, 1992), and *Epistemology and Cognition* (Harvard University Press, 1986).
[29] BonJour, *The Structure of Empirical Knowledge*, 37–57.   [30] Ibid. 41.

externalism about justification is thus equally successful in application to his own theory of justification. Since BonJour's requirement of cognitive accessibility seems to require that there be no gap between the appearance and the reality of justification, and since the difficulties involved in determining coherence open just such a gap, BonJour's coherentist account of justification fails to live up to the very standards that BonJour himself lays down.

The fact that the reliability of a belief-forming process is, in some sense, a factor external to the agent's system of beliefs, while coherence is, in some sense, internal to that system of beliefs does not in any way show that coherence is cognitively accessible or appropriately available to the agent. It is only by implicitly making the traditional Cartesian assumption that what is internal to the mind is wholly transparent to the agent that BonJour may slide from the claim that coherence is internal to an agent's beliefs to the claim that it is cognitively accessible to the agent in a way that objective reliability is not. Even if one endorses the traditional Cartesian claim about the special accessibility an agent has to the contents of his own mind, however, the claim of special access to logical relations among belief contents remains wildly implausible. The objective difficulty of determining coherence is simply undeniable.

This creates a problem not only for BonJour, but for all internalist versions of the coherence theory, and thus all views that would require that we recognize the coherence of our beliefs upon reflection. The motivation for internalist accounts, as BonJour clearly states, is to give an account of what is justified from an agent's own point of view. The objective coherence of an agent's beliefs, however, may be unavailable to an agent, and thus the dictates of coherence may fit the agent's point of view no better than the reliability of his processes of belief acquisition does. An internalist account of justification simply cannot be elaborated in terms of coherence.

But even this does not fully reveal the extent to which appeals to coherence create difficulties for any epistemology that would make reflective awareness a requirement for knowledge. Determining the coherence of a sizeable body of beliefs is not merely difficult; it is impossible. Since coherence requires consistency, let us consider once again the problems involved in determining the consistency of a large number of beliefs. The problems discussed thus far involved the difficulty human beings have in practice with determining consistency. But the problem here is not limited to human beings. Consider a device that checks a set of sentences in the propositional calculus for consistency by drawing up a truth-table. The number of lines on this truth-table will grow exponentially with the number of atomic sentence letters contained in the formulae to be tested. If there are only two atomic sentence letters, the truth-table will be four lines long; if there are five atomic sentence letters, the truth-table will be thirty-two lines long. In general, for n atomic sentence letters, the truth-table will be 2^n lines long. It should be clear that any such device runs into difficulties involving computational complexity quite quickly. As Christopher Cherniak notes,

Given the difficulties in individuating beliefs, it is not easy to estimate the number of logically independent atomic propositions in a typical human belief system, but 138 seems much too low—too 'small-minded'. Yet suppose that each line of the truth-table for the conjunction of all of these beliefs can be checked in the time a light ray takes to traverse the diameter of a proton, an appropriate cycle time for an ideal computer. At this maximum speed, a consistency test of this very modest belief system would require more time than the estimated twenty billion years from the dawn of the universe to the present.[31]

It is not simply that human beings have difficulty in determining the consistency of large sets of sentences. It is simply beyond the powers of any possible computational device to determine the consistency of a large set of sentences. In so far as coherence requires consistency, we can be sure that our beliefs are not the product of

[31] Christopher Cherniak, 'Computational Complexity and the Universal Acceptance of Logic', *Journal of Philosophy*, 81 (1984), 755–6.

mechanisms that determine coherence because such mechanisms are fundamentally impossible.[32]

The suggestion then that we ought to arrive at our beliefs by means of processes that recognize coherence proposes an ideal that human beings cannot meet and, indeed, that cannot be met by any possible computational device whatsoever. Nor is the problem simply one of determining consistency. The problem of computational complexity seems bound to arise for any holistic relation whatever operating over large fields of belief. It thus seems quite safe to say that any account that requires a reflective awareness of the coherence of one's beliefs is thereby setting a standard for knowledge that no one, and nothing, can meet. On any such account, no one ever knows anything at all.

Does this give us good reason to reject such an account of knowledge? BonJour argues that it does not.

It does seem clear . . . that it must at least be conceded that a completely accurate grasp of the degree of coherence of his system of beliefs is very unlikely to be available to the ordinary epistemic agent, and hence that here once again the ordinary agent's epistemic situation is only an approximation, and perhaps a fairly distant one, to an epistemic ideal.

The remaining question is whether there is anything implausible about any of these results. My basic claim is that one who falls short of a fully explicit grasp of his system of beliefs, or of the concept of coherence, or of the degree to which his system of beliefs is coherent, thereby fails to that extent to have a complete and fully explicit reason for thinking that those beliefs are true. And this seems to me in turn to make it reasonable to say that the justification we have is only approximate. But, at the same time, if the approximation is reasonably close, it is also easy enough to understand how common sense, neglectful as usual of fine distinction, might regard our beliefs as in many cases fully justified.[33]

---

[32] Thus Sosa's remark, quoted at the beginning of this chapter, that a 'reason-endowed being . . . automatically opts for the most coherent hypothesis', seems to lead to the conclusion that there are no reason-endowed beings.

[33] Laurence BonJour, 'Replies and Clarifications', in John Bender (ed.), *The Current State of the Coherence Theory* (Kluwer, 1989), 285.

What BonJour has to say here is, I believe, quite sensible if, as he notes 'the approximation is reasonably close', that is, if ordinary agents are able to come tolerably close to fulfilling the conditions he lays down for justification and knowledge. But surely the arguments just given show that the conditions coherence theorists such as BonJour require are not even approximately met. Consider the requirement that an agent have a reflective grasp of his entire corpus of beliefs. How close does anyone ever come to fulfilling this requirement? How many beliefs can one actually keep in mind at once? George Miller, in a famous paper directed at this question, has suggested that the capacity of working memory—which is where reflective awareness is plausibly located—is seven plus or minus two.[34] If Miller were mistaken by a factor of two, or three, or ten, or a hundred, or even a thousand, then BonJour's claim that the ordinary agent may at least approximate his requirements would still be very far from the truth. And it is quite clear that no agent can have a reflective awareness of even one hundred beliefs at a time. So the requirement that one have an explicit grasp of one's body of beliefs, by itself, shows that BonJour's standards are hopelessly out of reach for any real agent. The argument from computational complexity shows that the situation for assessments of coherence, even leaving aside an agent's ability to grasp the contents of his beliefs, is in very much the same situation. Human agents do not approximate BonJour's standards. The requirement that one have a reflective grasp of the coherence of one's beliefs puts justification and knowledge very far beyond us indeed.

Once this point is conceded, however, the suggestion that ordinary talk may be explained by the fact that common sense is 'neglectful as usual of fine distinctions' loses all plausibility. The distinction between what human beings are capable of and the standards BonJour requires for knowledge is not a matter of fine

---

[34] George Miller, 'The Magical Number Seven Plus or Minus Two: Some Limits on Our Capacity for Processing Information', in *The Psychology of Communication* (Basic Books, 1967).

distinctions or close approximations. Our ordinary talk about knowledge seems, on its face, to serve a useful purpose. Our attempts to distinguish between cases in which agents know and those in which they do not seem to succeed in marking an important distinction. But if BonJour is correct about the standards for knowledge, then all our ordinary judgments about agents actually knowing things are mistaken, and these judgments are mistaken not because they are only approximately true, even if strictly speaking false, but rather because they miss the mark by a country mile.

Now it does sometimes happen that ordinary agents are largely mistaken in their beliefs about some topics. Most people were, for a very long time, mistaken in their beliefs about the shape of the earth and the origin of species. Such examples are not hard to come by. But in this kind of case, those who successfully argued that commonly held beliefs on these subjects were not even close to true had a very large explanatory burden to bear. Why should we believe that knowledge requires the extraordinary degree of reflective awareness that BonJour insists upon? And why should we be willing to endorse the conclusion to which this inevitably leads, that the distinction we ordinarily draw, and which does so much work for us, between those who know something and those who do not, is entirely misguided, since no one ever knows anything at all? BonJour does not, it seems, meet the large explanatory burden with which such a position saddles him.

This is not, as I have urged, just a problem for BonJour. It is a problem for any coherence theorist who requires that agents have a reflective awareness of the coherence of their beliefs if they are to have knowledge. It is simply implausible to suggest that knowledge makes such demands upon us.

4.7 Idealized reflection: Foundationalist theories

Just as the coherence theory of justification may be presented in such a way as to require a reflective awareness of the coherence of one's beliefs, foundationalist theories of justification may also require that an agent be reflectively aware that his beliefs meet appropriate foundationalist standards. Internalist intuitions may, indeed, seem to demand such reflective awareness. An agent may certainly have beliefs that, as a matter of fact, exhibit the logical connections favored by some foundationalist theory without the agent having those beliefs in virtue of the holding of those connections. Such beliefs, it seems, would not constitute knowledge. But one natural account of what it is to hold beliefs in virtue of their exhibiting the appropriate foundationalist structure is just that the agent is reflectively aware that his beliefs conform to that structure. Any such foundationalist account of knowledge would set the standards for knowledge high enough that non-human animals could not meet it. Knowledge properly so-called, on this view, would be different in kind from 'mere animal knowledge'.

Such a foundationalist view would seem, at first glance, not to face the kinds of problems that analogous coherence theories suffer from. Because coherence is a relation among the totality of an agent's beliefs, coherence theories requiring reflective awareness of a belief's justificatory ground thereby require that an agent have a reflective grasp of his entire corpus of beliefs. Foundationalists do not, it seems, face a comparable difficulty precisely because their view of justification is not holistic. While the coherentist justification for any given belief inevitably involves every other belief an agent holds, foundationalist justification is, on its face, far more tractable. Similarly, while the coherence relation itself requires an understanding of logical relations among a set of beliefs so large as to create problems of computational complexity, typical foundationalist justifications are, by comparison, a model of simplicity. The problem of tractability thus seems to be one that does not arise for the foundationalist.

But any such apparent advantage for foundationalist accounts is entirely illusory because all current foundationalist accounts allow coherence considerations to play an important role in justification.

Consider, for example, Roderick Chisholm's foundationalism. No one is a more staunch defender of foundationalism than Chisholm. A central epistemic notion for Chisholm is that of a proposition being probable for an agent. On his view, 'If S accepts h and if h is not disconfirmed by S's total evidence, then h is probable for S.'[35] The appeal to an agent's total evidence is absolutely essential here, because the probability of a proposition cannot be determined by appeal to anything short of the totality of the agent's evidence. But if a foundationalist were to require a reflective grasp of the justificatory ground of his beliefs, the total evidence requirement would thereby require a reflective grasp of the agent's total evidence, something very far out of reach for any agent. This is not just a problem analogous to the one faced by the coherence theorist requiring reflective awareness of the grounds of an agent's belief; this is the very same problem.

Indeed, coherence enters Chisholm's system in an even more direct way, as it must for any foundationalist. Foundationalists reject the idea that coherence among an agent's beliefs is the only possible source of justification; but they do not reject the idea that coherence among beliefs that have some other prima-facie source of justification is itself an important justifier. Thus, Chisholm comments, 'Sometimes propositions *mutually support* each other. When this happens, each of the mutually supporting propositions may be said to add to the positive epistemic status of the other.'[36] But the size of the set of mutually supporting propositions may be large enough to elude any human agent's reflective grasp, and the logical relations among the propositions in such sets will thereby create problems of computational complexity. Foundationalists thus make requirements on justification that make a reflective grasp of the justificatory ground of a proposition fundamentally out of reach.

Initial appearances notwithstanding, foundationalist theories are in no better position than coherence theories to require a reflective

[35] Chisholm, *Theory of Knowledge*, 3rd edn. (Prentice-Hall, 1989), 63.
[36] Ibid. 69.

grasp of the grounds of justification. Both sorts of theory inevitably lead to a radical skepticism. But this is reason enough to reject any such theory. There is no reason to think that knowledge makes such radical demands on us.

4.8 Conclusion

The attempt to distinguish human knowledge from the knowledge of other animals by way of appeals to reflection is thus shown to be mistaken. Like the suggestion that human knowledge requires some sort of social metacognition, the suggestion that human knowledge requires reflection on one's justificatory grounds attempts to make some sort of metacognition a requirement for knowledge itself. Ironically, the attempt to show that human knowledge is thereby different in kind from the 'low-grade' knowledge of non-human animals leads to a conception of knowledge that even humans cannot come close to meeting. But this is not a reason for bemoaning some sort of deficiency on our part. Rather, it is a reason for thinking that this is not a viable conception of knowledge.

The conception of knowledge that we derived from the cognitive ethology literature, a reliabilist conception of knowledge, gives us the only viable account of what knowledge is. Human beings do have cognitive abilities that other animals do not, but this does not show in any way that human knowledge is different in kind from the knowledge of other animals. It is worth noting that bats, for example, have some sensory capabilities that other animals lack, and yet no one would suggest, on that basis, that the requirements for knowledge in bats are thereby different from the requirements for knowledge in other animals with different sensory capacities. A single set of standards for knowledge may be met by bats and sonarless animals. By the same token, human beings do have cognitive capacities that other animals lack. We may sometimes engage in social cognition of a sort that other animals cannot engage in, and we may sometimes reflect on our beliefs and their logical relations in ways of which other animals are incapable. The standards for knowledge, however, remain the same even across different sets of cognitive capacities. Human knowledge and the knowledge of non-human animals are not different in kind.

5

Normativity and Natural Knowledge

IN 1969, W. V. Quine advocated an approach to epistemological question that he called 'epistemology naturalized'. On Quine's view,

Epistemology, or something like it, simply falls into place as a chapter of psychology and hence of natural science. It studies a natural phenomenon, viz., a physical human subject. This human subject is accorded a certain experimentally controlled input—certain patterns of irradiation in assorted frequencies, for instance, and in the fullness of time the subject delivers as output a description of the three-dimensional world and its history. The relation between the meager input and the torrential output is a relation that we are prompted to study for somewhat the same reasons that always prompted epistemology; namely, in order to see how evidence relates to theory, and in what ways one's theory of nature transcends any available evidence.[1]

For many, this approach seemed to involve rejecting the normative dimension of epistemological theorizing, and, in so doing, abdicating at least one central role that epistemology has traditionally

---

[1] W. V. Quine, 'Epistemology Naturalized', in *Ontological Relativity and Other Essays* (Columbia University Press, 1969), 82–3.

played. Now it is true that nowhere in 'Epistemology Naturalized' does Quine specifically say that there is no normative role for epistemological theorizing to play; but passages such as the one quoted above surely do encourage this reading. If epistemology is to become nothing more than a chapter of psychology, or of cognitive ethology, or of the sciences generally, then, on one straightforward account of what the sciences are all about, the resulting discipline will become merely descriptive, and thereby lose all normative force.

Quine has since clarified his account of naturalistic epistemology, and he has repudiated the suggestion that there is no place for normativity within epistemological theorizing.

Naturalization of epistemology does not jettison the normative and settle for the indiscriminate description of ongoing procedures. For me normative epistemology is a branch of engineering. It is the technology of truth-seeking, or, in a more cautiously epistemological term, prediction . . . There is no question here of ultimate value, as in morals; it is a matter of efficacy for an ulterior end, truth or prediction. The normative here, as elsewhere in engineering, becomes descriptive when the terminal parameter is expressed.[2]

This passage is admirably clear on the point that a naturalistic epistemology does not abandon normative theorizing. It is, however, far less clear than one might like on the source of this normativity. Once we accept truth as our goal, there are, clearly, some empirical questions to be answered in what Quine calls the 'technology of truth-seeking', and questions of this sort have occupied many who think of themselves as naturalistic epistemologists. But how is it that truth acquires this status as our goal and thereby confers normative force on the recommendations to pursue certain strategies of belief acquisition and retention, namely, those which are conducive to achieving it? Does Quine mean to be making a

    [2] W. V. Quine, 'Reply to Morton White', in Lewis Hahn and Paul Schilpp (eds.), *The Philosophy of W. V. Quine* (Open Court, 1986), 664–5.

sociological observation here, that many people do in fact have this goal? Or is there some deeper fact about true belief that somehow recommends it to us? It is especially important to address these questions when many in the naturalistic tradition have, on the one hand, suggested that truth is not the only goal of our epistemic activity,[3] or, on the other, that the goal of truth should be abandoned in favor of other goals, such as fitness[4] or the totality of things we value exclusive of truth.[5] If we are to be in any position rationally to adjudicate among these competing views, we cannot rest content with Quine's seemingly innocent suggestion that epistemic norms 'become descriptive when the terminal parameter is expressed', for we need to know what the source of this terminal parameter is. What, ultimately, is the source of epistemic normativity?

This question about the source of epistemic normativity is not just a question for epistemologists of a naturalistic turn of mind. In so far as epistemologists endorse epistemic norms, it is incumbent upon them to explain the source of this normativity. How is it that epistemic norms come to have their normative force? What we are looking for here is not necessarily a naturalistically acceptable answer to this question, but any acceptable answer. What we need is an account of the source of epistemic normativity that does not make a mystery of it.

I begin by considering a semantic approach to this problem implicit in the work of Alvin Goldman. I argue in sect. 5.1 that this kind of approach cannot provide us with a satisfying solution. In sect. 5.2, I explain how norms might be grounded in desire, and in the sections that follow, I pursue a number of different ways of working out this suggestion. All such accounts make epistemic norms a

[3] See e.g. Hartry Field, 'Realism and Relativism', *Journal of Philosophy*, 79 (1982), 553–67; Alvin Goldman, *Epistemology and Cognition* (Harvard University Press, 1986); and Catherine Elgin, 'The Epistemic Efficacy of Stupidity', *Synthese*, 74 (1988), 297–311.

[4] See William Lycan, ' "Is" and "Ought" in Cognitive Science', *Behavioral and Brain Sciences*, 4 (1981), 344–5, and *Judgment and Justification* (Cambridge University Press, 1988), esp. ch. 7.

[5] Stephen Stich, *The Fragmentation of Reason* (MIT Press, 1990).

variety of hypothetical imperative: they tell us how we should acquire our beliefs if we meet certain conditions. Accounts of this sort run the risk of being parochial. If the conditions are met by few people, then epistemic norms should be of little interest to most of us. Even if the conditions are met by many, norms construed as hypothetical imperatives seem inevitably to lack the universality that we want our epistemic norms to have.

The account I believe to be most promising, while a species of the hypothetical imperatives approach, nevertheless makes epistemic norms universal. I argue that there are certain substantive constraints that we will want our cognitive systems to meet simply on the condition that we value anything at all. Since everyone, indeed, every animal with beliefs and desires, values something or other, this condition is universally met; the imperatives to have cognitive systems meeting my constraints thus apply to all who have cognitive systems. I argue that this kind of account of normativity flows naturally from the account of knowledge offered in Ch. 2. Such an account provides, I believe, much of what we want in an account of the source of epistemic normativity. I am not at all convinced that it is possible to give an account of epistemic norms that provides more than this.

5.1 A semantic source for epistemic normativity?

I want to begin by examining the way in which Alvin Goldman makes room for normativity in his naturalistic epistemology. Although Goldman's account is not the sort with which Quine would be sympathetic, it provides, for many, an extremely attractive way of explaining the source of epistemic norms.

Goldman is rightly famous for urging epistemologists to make more room for empirical concerns in general, and psychological concerns in particular, within their epistemological theorizing. But in *Epistemology and Cognition*, empirical concerns play no role at all in explaining the source of epistemic normativity. In spite of his urging that 'epistemology should be a multidisciplinary affair, not the province of pure, *a priori* philosophy',[6] Goldman makes room for an important a priori component in his epistemology, and it is precisely here that epistemic normativity gets its footing.

In what Goldman conceives of as the foundational part of epistemology, we engage in autonomous enquiry into the meaning of various epistemic terms. We do this by way of testing proposed analyses against our intuitions, and we thereby attempt to capture our ordinary concept of, for example, justification or knowledge.[7] Thus, Goldman says, 'I suggest that the meaning of the term "justified" (in its epistemic sense) is fixed by certain things that we *presume* about the world, whether we are right or not.'[8]

At this foundational level of enquiry, what the world is actually like is irrelevant, for we are attempting to discover the contours of our ordinary concept of, say, justification, and this concept is constructed against a backdrop of assumptions about the world.[9] We are not attempting to discover whether this concept is, in some sense to be specified, adequate or accurate; we are merely attempting to discover what the concept is. Conceptual analysis does not require empirical information about the world around us. This is, I believe, a very familiar conception of what at least one part of epistemology is all about. Goldman's break with traditional epistemology in *Epistemology and Cognition*, and the features of that account that make it a variety of naturalism, are not to be found here. Rather, they are to be found in Goldman's insistence that this is not all there is to epistemology, and in his important and distinctive ways of illuminating the contributions that psychology makes to epistemological projects of obvious importance.

---

[6] Goldman, *Epistemology and Cognition*, 1.

[7] Notice that this is exactly what Bealer refers to as the 'standard justificatory procedure' in philosophy. See sect. 1.2 above.

[8] *Epistemology and Cognition*, 108. [9] See ibid. 107.

Nevertheless, it is in the foundational part of epistemology, in the part that is investigated by examining our concepts, that epistemic normativity is located. The terms of epistemic appraisal are evaluative terms: to say that a belief is justified, or that it is a case of knowledge, is to say that it is good in some sense: 'epistemology is an evaluative, or normative, or critical discipline. Let me now address the possible scope and nature of such evaluation. First, what do we mean by "evaluation," or "norm"? We mean a judgment that pronounces something good or bad, right or wrong, proper or improper, and the like.'[10] Moreover, we discover through conceptual analysis what conditions must be satisfied if a belief is to be justified, or a case of knowledge, or whatever. It is thus a matter of conceptual analysis both that the class of justified beliefs are good, right, or proper, and that they are identified by certain empirical conditions (roughly, being produced by processes that are truth-conducive). Suppose then that someone were to ask what makes truth-conduciveness a good thing: 'What is good', this person asks, 'about justified belief so understood?' Goldman seems committed to the following answer. To be justified is simply to be something good; this is a matter of the meaning of the term. Similarly, and to a first approximation, for a belief to be justified simply is for it to be the product of a truth-conducive process; this, too, is a matter of the meaning of the term. Thus, it is merely a matter of the meaning of the term 'justified' that truth-conduciveness is a good thing. A similar argument may, of course, be constructed for other epistemic terms of approval. Normative force seems to derive from semantic considerations alone.

Now there is something terribly unsatisfying about this. Imagine someone, such as Stephen Stich, who claims that conduciveness to truth is of no value at all; that a belief that is the product of a truth-conducive process is not, in virtue of that very fact, a good belief to have. On Stich's view, it is not merely that truth by itself does not

---

[10] *Epistemology and Cognition*, 20.

make a proposition worthy of belief; rather, the truth of a belief, or the truth-conduciveness of the process that produced it, does not even count in its favor. Now if Stich were to confront Goldman and ask why he should favor true beliefs, or beliefs produced by truth-conducive processes, it seems that Goldman should offer him the semantic argument above. It also seems that this should not convince Stich at all.

Indeed, this is exactly what Stich says. Stich is concerned that even if Goldman has given the proper conceptual analysis of our epistemic terms, the fact that he has uncovered the proper conceptual analysis carries no normative force. In particular, as Stich points out, suppose there were another culture whose epistemic terms embodied a different set of standards. Suppose that in this other culture beliefs meeting different conditions were approved of. What reason is there to approve of beliefs meeting our conditions rather than those meeting the conditions of this other culture? It will hardly do to point out that this is what out terms mean. As Stich puts it,

imagine that we have located some exotic culture that does in fact exploit cognitive processes very different from our own and that the notions of epistemic evaluation embedded in their language also differ from ours. Suppose further that the cognitive processes prevailing in that culture accord quite well with *their* evaluative notions, while the cognitive processes prevailing in our culture accord quite well with *ours*. Would any of this be of any help at all in deciding which cognitive processes we should use? Without some reason to think that one set of evaluative notions was preferable to the other, it seems clear that for most of us it would be of no help at all.[11]

What Goldman says on this score only serves to underline the difficulty of the position he is in. Goldman offers a reliability account of justification and knowledge, and there are a number of different ways to explicate the notion of reliability. Here is what Goldman says about his preferred account, the normal worlds account:

[11] Stich, *The Fragmentation of Reason*, 92–3.

My proposal to judge reliability by reference to normal worlds is made in the spirit of trying to elucidate the *ordinary* conception of justifiedness. I am prepared to be persuaded that this ordinary conception can be improved upon. I would lend a receptive ear to proposals to 'regiment' the conception of justifiedness so as to judge rightness by reliability in the *actual* world, or by reliability in the possible world of the belief in question. Either of these approaches might seem preferable from a systematic or theoretical point of view. Nonetheless, they do not seem to be what is implied by the ordinary conception as it stands; and that is all I am currently trying to capture.[12]

When Goldman acknowledges that conceptions of justifiedness other than the ordinary one might be preferable to it, he is granting Stich's point. Semantic considerations alone thus cannot explain the normative force of epistemic terms. In particular, the kind of semantic analysis that Goldman practices cannot explain the force of his own remark that he might find standards different from the ones captured by our ordinary use of epistemic terms 'preferable', for, of course, only the very standards we have would be recommended by the standards we currently employ. What we really want to know, as Stich rightly urges, is what standards we ought to have, and semantic analysis cannot answer this question. Semantic arguments cannot explain the source of epistemic normativity.

Goldman has recently rejected his suggestion that an a priori investigation of our ordinary concepts can tell us about the nature of justification and knowledge,[13] but not because he rejects the enterprise of conceptual analysis. Goldman has suggested instead that conceptual analysis is not to be understood as an a priori discipline; it is to be investigated by straightforwardly empirical means. Goldman's current psychologized account of the meanings of terms, where lexical items are said to have psychologically real

[12] Goldman, *Epistemology and Cognition*, 109.

[13] Alvin Goldman, 'Psychology and Philosophical Analysis', *Proceedings of the Aristotelian Society*, 89 (1988), 195–209, and Goldman and Joel Pust, 'Philosophical Theory and Intuitional Evidence', in M. DePaul and W. Ramsey (eds.), *Rethinking Intuition* (Rowman & Littlefield, 1998), 179–97.

semantic representations, fits in more easily, I believe, with his overall naturalistic orientation. It is important to see, however, that this kind of move does nothing to solve the problem Stich poses. Whether the meanings of our terms are discovered by a priori investigation or by psychological experimentation is simply irrelevant to the issue under discussion. The fact remains that semantic considerations alone cannot explain the source of the normative force of epistemic terms. Whatever I might mean by the term 'justified', and whatever I might currently approve of, there is a substantive question to be asked about why I should approve of certain sorts of beliefs, and this question is not answered by pointing out what it is I mean by the term 'justified'. Goldman's accounts, both old and new, are in no position to explain the source of epistemic normativity.[14]

5.2 Grounding epistemic norms in desire

Any account that does explain the source of epistemic normativity must explain how it is that epistemic claims have normative force. If you tell me that a belief of mine is unjustified, this gives me reason to give up that belief. The epistemic claim is something about which I should care, and an account of the source of epistemic norms must explain why it is that I should care about such things. Since having a desire for something gives one a reason to care about it, it is well worth considering whether desire might serve as the source of epistemic normativity.

There are a number of different ways in which desire might be pressed into service as the source of epistemic norms. I briefly chart the territory here, and in the sections that follow I examine the various possibilities in greater detail.

[14] In 'Epistemic Folkways and Scientific Epistemology', in *Liaisons: Philosophy Meets the Cognitive and Social Sciences* (MIT Press, 1992), 155–75, Goldman makes room for the revision of our 'folk concepts' of justification and knowledge, thereby leaving room for the kinds of concerns urged here.

Stich's account of the relationship between epistemic normativity and desire is certainly the boldest. Stich suggests that epistemic evaluation is grounded in desires for whatever we intrinsically value. Thus,

In evaluating systems of cognitive processes, the system to be preferred is the one that would be most likely to achieve those things that are intrinsically valued by the person whose interests are relevant to the purposes of evaluation. In most cases, the relevant person will be the one who is or might be using the system. So, for example, if the issue at hand is the evaluation of Smith's system of cognitive processes in comparison with some actual or hypothetical alternative, the system that comes out higher on the pragmatist account of cognitive evaluation is the one that is most likely to lead to the things that Smith finds intrinsically valuable . . . there is no mystery why Smith should care about the outcome of this evaluation.[15]

In light of the diversity of the things that we find intrinsically valuable, this kind of position leads to a form of relativism: the standards that determine what is epistemically right for me are likely to be quite different from the standards that determine what is epistemically right for you. No sense can be made of any attempt to adjudicate among these standards.

Grounding epistemic norms in desire does not, of course, require this radical a position, nor does it require any sort of relativism. Those who seek to avoid relativism in epistemic evaluation, while simultaneously grounding norms in desire, will construe norms as imperatives that apply given that certain conditions are met. Such a view may take any of the following three forms: (1) imperatives may be endorsed that are simply conditional on having certain desires or goals, while acknowledging that these goals are not universally shared; relativity is thereby avoided at the price of a loss of universality; (2) it may be argued that although epistemic imperatives are conditional upon having certain particular goals, these goals are in fact universally held; and (3) it may be argued that epistemic imperatives are conditional upon having any goals at all.

[15] Stich, *The Fragmentation of Reason*, 131–2.

I proceed as follows. In sect. 5.3, I examine the view that epistemic norms are imperatives that apply given that one has a certain particular desire or goal; this encompasses both possibilities (1) and (2) above. I argue that the first of these views, which abandons universality, is not implausible, but that the cost of abandoning universality is not negligible either. The second of these views, however, which would have us regain universality, is extremely implausible. In sect. 5.4, I consider Stich's view that we should instead allow the totality of our concerns to dictate epistemic norms. I argue that Stich's pragmatic view is untenable. In coming to understand why this view is untenable, however, we are provided with the basis for an account of epistemic norms that explains them as imperatives contingent upon having any goals whatever. This view is, I believe, extremely promising, and I examine it further in sect. 5.5.

5.3 Epistemic norms as grounded in particular desires

Let us then consider the suggestion that epistemic norms be understood as imperatives contingent upon having certain goals. This is, perhaps, the most natural way of understanding Quine's comment that 'There is no question here of ultimate value, as in morals; it is a matter of efficacy for an ulterior end, truth or prediction.' What is the best way to fill out this view?

It might be thought that as long as epistemic norms are being construed in this way we may simply stipulate any end for epistemic activity we like, and, precisely because the end is merely stipulated, it itself requires no justification.[16] Thus, if Quine is interested in the extent to which belief-producing processes are truth-conducive, he may certainly evaluate them in that way. Others who value the truth as well will find this illuminating; those who do not will find this

---

[16] I myself do not believe that this is a proper account of what is involved in stipulation, but because so many use that term as if it carried with it no requirement of justification, I will follow that practice here.

kind of evaluation of less interest. Similarly, if someone wants to evaluate epistemic activity from the point of view of its conduciveness to truth plus something else, or just something else entirely, that person is free to do so. The norms that issue from such schemes of evaluation are merely directed at select audiences. It should be noted that for those, like Quine, who choose a goal that is very widely held, the interest of their normative scheme is assured. Since many people do clearly care about the truth of their beliefs,[17] Quinean epistemic norms, construed as imperatives contingent upon valuing truth, will carry normative force for a great many people. This would surely explain much of what needs to be explained about the force of epistemic norms.

Although this is certainly one way to fill out the view that epistemic norms are hypothetical imperatives, I do not believe that this way of filling it out does justice to the concerns of many of those involved in epistemological theorizing.

There have, after all, been debates about the ends toward which epistemic norms are directed. Some, like Quine, favor truth and nothing else. Some have urged that the goal of truth must be balanced against other important goals, such as comprehensiveness and speed. Still others have suggested that the goal of truth should be dropped entirely in favor of, for example, biological fitness. How are we to understand these debates?

If the ends that epistemic norms posit are merely stipulated in the way described above, there is no room for substantive debate among these different schemes of evaluation. Epistemic activity may be evaluated for its conduciveness to various ends, some of which are widely held and some of which are more parochial; but these different schemes of evaluation are not competitors. On this account, it is not as if those who offer different schemes were each trying to characterize a single notion. The problem with this account, of course, is

[17] Or at least believe that they do. Stich denies that many people really do attach intrinsic value to the truth of their beliefs.

that those who offer different schemes of evaluation typically have seen other schemes of evaluation as competitors. The tenor of this debate suggests that the different parties to it believe themselves to be attempting to characterize a single notion, with some parties to the debate getting it right and others getting it wrong. Now it is certainly possible that the various parties to this debate are simply confused, and this, of course, is what the stipulation account suggests. But it is at least worth exploring whether there might be some account available here that would lend substance to these debates rather than merely dismissing them as conceptual confusions.

Fortunately, there is. The various parties to this debate do not act as if they are merely offering their favorite end as a way of giving substance to epistemic evaluation. Instead, there are activities in which humans are frequently involved, and the favored ends are offered as ways of making sense of and accounting for these activities. For many epistemologists, it is making sense of science that is at issue. Truth is thus frequently offered as at least one of the goals of epistemic activity because science is seen as a paradigm of such activity, and we can understand what science is about when we see it as motivated by a desire for truth. To the extent that this makes sense of scientific activity, it thereby makes sense of a system of evaluation that measures success by its conduciveness to truth. There is room for substantive disagreement here when others agree about the kind of activity they wish to evaluate, and yet disagree about the kinds of motivations that make sense of it. Norms that arise from such evaluations remain merely hypothetical, for they are contingent upon valuing the activity that is made sense of by the indicated concerns. On this view, then, the suggestion that these norms are hypothetical does not make them entirely idiosyncratic, for the activity that gives rise to them may be very widely valued; nor does it make substantive disagreement about them impossible, for there are substantive questions about what the aims or goals of the activity actually are.

This is, I believe, the most plausible version of the view that epistemic norms are imperatives contingent upon valuing certain particular ends.[18] Nevertheless, there can be no doubt that it leaves out much that might be desired in an account of epistemic normativity. Why is it, for example, that science is so frequently seen as a paradigm activity from which epistemic norms might be derived? On the account just given, the answer must be merely that many people do value it. Those who wish to say more, for example, that those who do not value science nevertheless ought to, do not see the norms that issue from scientific practice as merely optional. It would certainly be nice if we could have an account of epistemic normativity that gave substance to the suspicion that the force of such norms is not so easily avoided.

It is important to note as well that any attempt to gain universal applicability by appeal to goals that all humans in fact have will almost certainly run afoul of the facts. Human beings are a very diverse lot; some of us are quite strange. It is hard to imagine making a plausible case for any particular goal or activity that is genuinely universally valued. There is good reason to believe, at a minimum, that science is not such an activity. I think it is safe to say that anyone who attempts to derive universally applicable norms in this way, namely by combining hypothetical imperatives with particular universally shared goals, has a very substantial burden of proof to meet.

5.4 Epistemic norms and the totality of things we value

Let us turn then to Stich's view, that epistemic evaluation is just the determination of the extent to which our cognitive states or processes are conducive to the totality of things we value intrinsically.

---

[18] Room should be made as well for interaction between views about the goals that make sense of an activity and the activity itself. On discovering that an activity I value makes sense only relative to certain goals, I may modify the activity itself by modifying the goals. This kind of reflective equilibrium account fits well with the view of norms as imperatives contingent upon having certain goals.

What is the attraction of a view such as this? As Stich indicates, such a view has an important advantage over semantic views like Goldman's. Stich is able to explain straightforwardly why it is that anyone should care about the epistemic status of his cognitive states and processes, which would not be possible with semantic views. Precisely by identifying cognitive evaluation with conduciveness to things one cares about, Stich assures that everyone will care about the outcome of cognitive evaluation. The extent to which one should care about cognitive evaluation on Stich's view, however, may be more a source of difficulty than a point in its favor.

If someone tells me that a belief of mine is unjustified, this seems to me to count against my holding it. On Stich's view, however, this is not merely one consideration against it; it provides a conclusive reason for rejecting it. The judgment that a belief is epistemically unacceptable is, on Stich's view, no different from the judgment that all things considered, it is unacceptable; for on Stich's view epistemic evaluation already takes account of everything an agent values. Now there are two things that are quite strange about this result, and I believe that they are related.

1. We commonly assume that epistemic evaluation is only one kind of evaluation among many. A candidate belief may fare badly when it comes to epistemic evaluation, but fare well when it comes to various other kinds of evaluation, say, aesthetic or moral. Now it is not that Stich has no room for other kinds of evaluation; he clearly does. Given his strategy of gaining normative force by tying norms to desires, these other norms would presumably derive from desires an agent might have. But if these norms are to be any different from epistemic norms, as surely they must, then they will derive their normative force from some proper subset of the agent's desires for things to which he attaches intrinsic value, rather than the totality of such desires, as is the source of epistemic norms. But if Stich has room for legitimate evaluation that derives only from a subset of an agent's desires, why is it that he insists on tying epistemic norms to

the totality of an agent's desires for things to which he attaches intrinsic value? Isn't epistemic evaluation, like many other kinds, more plausibly viewed as directed by only certain concerns and not others? It seems strange that epistemic evaluation should be so all-encompassing. Thus, for example, it seems that I might recognize that having a certain belief would be epistemically ill-advised, and yet have good reason, all things considered, for trying to come to have the belief. If I could assure world peace by committing some epistemic impropriety, surely it would be worth the price. By identifying epistemic propriety with all-things-considered judgments, Stich makes this thought self-contradictory.

2. This leads to my second point. What is it, on Stich's account, that makes epistemic evaluation epistemic? I recognize that the objects of evaluation, namely cognitive states and processes, lend some epistemic flavor to this mode of evaluation. But these same objects may be evaluated from, for example, an aesthetic perspective. The mere fact that we are evaluating beliefs does not make our evaluation an epistemic one. And the range of desires people have surely does not do much to lend an epistemic flavor to the evaluation relative to all one's concerns. Stich's own examples here do not help his case. His chief examples of things one might intrinsically value are health, happiness, and the well-being of one's children.[19] It is hard to see how evaluation relative to these concerns is rightly termed epistemic.

Indeed, it seems to me that the natural way to describe Stich's pragmatic view is to say that it is eliminitivist about epistemic evaluation: there is nothing distinctively epistemic about the kind of evaluation Stich proposes. If this is correct, then Stich's pragmatic approach falls outside the purview of this chapter, for I am interested in finding out what room can be made for genuinely epistemic evaluation. If Stich's account should prove correct, it would be because there is no room for such evaluation.

[19] Stich, *The Fragmentation of Reason*, 131.

I do want to suggest, however, that Stich's position is not available to those seeking an account of epistemic evaluation, even as a fallback position. More importantly, by seeing how Stich's view fails, we are given a basis for a more substantive and satisfying account of epistemic evaluation. In order to see why this is so, we must imagine that we are actually trying to implement a Stichean evaluation. Here is how Stich tells us to do this.

To assess the comparative merits of a pair of cognitive systems that a person might exploit requires that we compute the expected value of adopting each system. To do that, we must determine the probability of each option leading to various possible outcomes and then multiply those probabilities by the cardinal number indices of the values we have assigned the outcomes. The consequences that are important for a pragmatic evaluation will be things that the person in question takes to be intrinsically valuable.[20]

Stich bases this account on standard cost-benefit models of decision. But the presuppositions of cost-benefit calculations undermine Stich's attempt to turn this into an account of cognitive evaluation.

Consider an unproblematic case in which the cost-benefit approach is applied. If I am deciding between two toasters and I wish to use the cost-benefit model, I will begin by determining the consequences of buying each of the candidate toasters. I assign values to each of these consequences, and I do some simple arithmetic. The toaster that has the higher expected value is the toaster I should buy.

In doing all of this, I make use of my cognitive system. I need to figure out the relevant consequences; I need to assign values to each of them; I need to do some arithmetic. The cost-benefit account assumes that these will be done accurately, otherwise the fact that one toaster is assigned a higher number by this procedure is of no interest. So it is assumed that my cognitive system is generating truths about the toasters,[21] truths about what I value, and accurately computing certain arithmetic functions. These assumptions are

[20] Ibid. 134.
[21] Or accurate probabilities. This complication will not help Stich.

perfectly legitimate ones to make when trying to devise a decision procedure for the purchase of toasters. It is how we figure out which toaster better serves our interests, whatever those interests may be.[22]

Now Stich proposes that we evaluate cognitive systems in much the same way. We do not, Stich tells us, value truth, but we do value a great many things: health, happiness, the welfare of our children, and so on. So in evaluating our cognitive systems, we should choose those that favor things that we value (rather than those that favor truth), just as we do when choosing among toasters.

Now it will not be unfair to Stich to assume that cognitive systems that are effective in producing happiness and so on are quite different, both in their inferences and in the beliefs they ultimately produce, from cognitive systems that are effective in producing truths. Indeed, it would be miraculous if all cognitive systems produced inferences and beliefs in very much the same way, regardless of the ends they were effective in serving. Moreover, were this the case, it would rob Stich's position of its interest, for Stich means to be endorsing systems very different from those that are favored by truth-based accounts. So we may safely assume, without unfairness to Stich, that those systems that satisfy his epistemic standards produce beliefs which, by and large, are not true.

Now it seems to me that if we accept a cognitive system of the sort Stich commends, we will have undermined our project of satisfying our desires, whatever those desires may be. For let us imagine now that we are faced, once again, with the prospect of choosing between two toasters, and let us suppose that we do not have a cognitive system that is effective in getting at the truth. Let us instead

---

[22] Stich would actually deny this. It is, indeed, the burden of ch. 5 of *The Fragmentation of Reason* to argue that the notion of truth is an idiosyncratic notion, of no cognitive significance. I cannot possibly do justice to Stich's argument here. Those who favor cost-benefit analyses, however, have traditionally made the assumptions I attribute to them in the text. It would be interesting to see precisely what a full-blown Stichean reconstruction of cost-benefit analyses would look like. It is not at all clear that such an account can be coherently provided.

suppose that we possess a cognitive system that favors happiness, for we are terribly simple folk and care about nothing but happiness. In choosing between the two toasters, once again, we must figure out the consequences of the two purchases; we must assign values to each of them; we must do some arithmetic. If we performed this calculation by using a cognitive system that gave us true beliefs, we would thereby be informed about the actual consequences of purchasing each toaster, what it is we actually value, and the extent to which these consequences actually produce those things we value. We would thus come to know which toaster better serves our interests, whatever those interests may be.

But Stich does not commend such a cognitive system to us. Instead, he endorses cognitive systems that themselves serve our interests. And we have seen that we may, without unfairness to Stich, assume that such cognitive systems produce very different beliefs than systems which are truth-conducive. But this means that when the happiness-conducive cognitive system is turned to the task of toaster evaluation, it will not tell us what the actual consequences are of purchasing each toaster; instead it will tell us what we would be happiest to believe the consequences to be. Similarly, the happiness-conducive cognitive system will not accurately tell us what it is we value; it will tell us instead what it is we would be happiest to believe that we value. Finally, it will not tell us accurately what will, all things considered, serve our interests, but instead what would make us happiest to believe will, all things considered, serve our interests. As we have seen, it is not unfair to Stich to assume that in each of these cases the happiness-conducive system will generate different results from the truth-conducive system. To put the point only slightly differently, the happiness-conducive system will not tell us which toaster will actually make us happier. Allowing our cognitive systems to be determined by the totality of our interests exclusive of truth thus undermines our ability to make choices, outside the cognitive realm, that are conducive to those very interests.

It is thus safe to say, I believe, that Stich's proposed method of epistemic evaluation does not do the job it was meant to do. Ironically enough, Stich's attempt to devise a pragmatic scheme of cognitive evaluation runs into difficulty precisely where a pragmatic account should be strongest: namely, in allowing us to act so as to serve whatever interests we may care about. It is only by evaluating cognitive systems without regard for the effect such evaluation would have on our actions that Stich is able to endorse the cognitive systems he does. It seems that someone who cares about acting in a way that furthers the things he cares about, and that includes all of us, has pragmatic reasons to favor a cognitive system that is effective in generating truths, whether he otherwise cares about the truth or not. We should thus adopt a method of cognitive evaluation that endorses truth-conducive processes.

Let me make one final point. The criticism of the last paragraph may suggest that I believe Stich's method of cognitive evaluation could be effective in initiating modifications in cognitive systems, and that difficulties arise only when the outputs of those cognitive systems are used in evaluating choices for action. Now this would be cold comfort to Stich or any other pragmatist, but I do not believe that Stich's system of evaluation would work on even this extremely limited scale. Imagine someone evaluating his own cognitive system to see, as Stich suggests we ought, the extent to which it is conducive to the things he cares about. For reasons like those just presented, such an evaluation will only be accurate if the agent uses a cognitive system that generates truths. If the agent abandons such a cognitive system in favor of some non-truth-conducive system, then when the agent is prompted to re-evaluate his cognitive system relative to others, he will not accurately determine the comparative merits of the two systems, even relative to his own standards. Having abandoned a truth-conducive cognitive system for one that satisfies the many things he values, he will be no more able to assess accurately the merits of his cognitive system than he will be able to assess accurately the merits of toasters. So Stich's system of cognitive evaluation could not be put to work on successive cognitive evaluations, even if one were wholly unconcerned about the ways in which beliefs bear on action.

In actual practice, of course, our cognitive systems are not perfectly truth-conducive. There is some reason to think, however, that they do tolerably well when it comes to truth-conduciveness. The hope is that by applying standards of truth-conduciveness by our own lights, we may, over time, more nearly realize those standards that we seek to attain. While there is certainly no guarantee that we will be able to do this, neither is it an idle hope that an approximately truth-conducive system will be able to improve its own reliability when it is reflexively turned to that task. Notice, in particular, that scientific realists are committed to a claim that is, structurally, quite similar: that science may improve its accuracy over time through application of its own methods to methodological questions, thereby trading approximately true theories for ones that are more nearly true. While much work still remains to be done in showing why we should expect such progress, the claim that approximately truth-conducive methods will converge in this way is surely far more plausible than any comparable claim about happiness-conducive methods or any of the others that might be substituted for those that aim at the truth.

5.5 Epistemic norms as universal hypothetical imperatives

The argument I just gave against Stich seems to provide the basis for an account of the source of epistemic norms that would allow, on the one hand, that they are derived from our desires in a way that removes any mystery surrounding them, and, on the other, that they are universal in their applicability and not merely contingent upon having certain values. Since this seems to provide us with almost everything we could reasonably want in an account of epistemic norms, it is necessary to examine this view with some care.

The problem for Stich arose because we need to make evaluations of alternative courses of action and, whatever we care about, we need these evaluations to be done accurately, i.e. by a cognitive system that generates truths. If we have been making revisions in our cognitive system that make it unable to serve this function, then by our own standards we will have done ourselves a disservice. It is thus of the first importance that our cognitive systems remain suitable for the purpose of performing the relevant cost-benefit calculations. And what this requires is that our cognitive systems be accurate, that is, that they reliably get at the truth.

This suggests that epistemic evaluation takes on a special role. Such evaluation cannot be, as Stich suggests, all-things-considered evaluation; it cannot be so all-encompassing. Precisely because our cognitive systems are required to perform evaluations relative to our many concerns, and to perform these evaluations accurately, the standards by which we evaluate these cognitive systems themselves must remain insulated from most of what we intrinsically value, whatever we may value. This provides a reason to care about the truth whatever we may otherwise care about. It also provides us with a reason to evaluate our cognitive systems by their conduciveness to truth. And this is precisely what epistemic evaluation is all about. Truth plays a pre-eminent role here.

Have I assumed here that epistemic evaluation is measured by conduciveness to truth and nothing else? I have not. I have argued that truth is pre-eminent here; that any account of epistemic evaluation that does not give truth a central role to play is inadequate. There may still be a good deal of room for other factors to play a role. My argument for the importance of truth turned on its being implicated in certain cost-benefit calculations; the calculations that we need to perform in making choices among alternative courses of action must be done accurately. But various goals other than truth are likely to be implicated in this task as well. A system of evaluation that was perfectly accurate but could not perform its evaluations in real time[23] would be of little value. The task of evaluation thus brings with it certain demands. There is room for substantive disagreement about just what those demands are. And it is just this kind of discussion that lends substance to debates about the dimensions of epistemic evaluation.

5.6 Description and prescription

The account of knowledge I defended in Ch. 2 locates knowledge in the world as a natural kind. On this view, we are committed to the existence of knowledge because knowledge does causal work and talk of knowledge plays an explanatory role in our theories. We are thus committed to the existence of knowledge, on this view, for the same kinds of reasons that we are committed to the existence of quarks and quasars, gold and gophers. Knowledge is a feature of the world.

But any such approach to knowledge, it may seem, will inevitably rob it of its normative force. Even if there is some natural category that plays a causal role in explaining a variety of phenomena, such as fitness and goal-satisfying behavior, this gives us no reason to think that this particular natural phenomenon is the same as the object of philosophical investigation. Philosophers are interested in a category that has normative implications. To say that a belief is an item of knowledge is to praise it in a certain way; it is to approve of it as meeting our cognitive ideals; it is to recommend it. Even if there is a natural category that plays a certain important causal role, and so an adequate description of the world must recognize the existence of such a category, the kind of knowledge philosophers are interested in is not rightly thought of as such a kind. In a word, philosophical talk of knowledge is not merely descriptive; it is prescriptive. And prescriptive categories need not answer to anything that actually

---

[23] Christopher Cherniak has illuminating things to say about this issue in his *Minimal Rationality*, (MIT Press, 1986).

exists in the world at all. The categories in which we couch our normative theories—our view of what the world ought to be like—need not be held hostage to any description of the actual causal structure of the world.[24]

The vast gulf that this objection presupposes between the descriptive and the prescriptive, between the natural and the normative, is not, of course, any part of the naturalistic world-view defended in this book. While naturalists are in no way committed to a normative theory that simply approves of the world as it currently is, neither can they allow for normative categories that are so far removed from an accurate description of deep features of the causal structure of the world, as is assumed in this objection. Consider the cognitive ethologist's notion of knowledge. It gets its purchase on the causal structure of the world because knowledge so conceived is conducive to fitness; such knowledge is instrumental in producing behavior that satisfies a creature's biologically given needs. Is it any wonder that we should value such a condition, that we should see it as worthy of our pursuit? Knowledge is of extraordinary instrumental value, for it allows us to achieve our biologically given goals, as well as our more idiosyncratic individual goals, whatever those goals may be. This makes it a condition that is universally valuable.[25]

It is not, of course, mere coincidence that this particular normative category should match a category that is embedded in a causal / descriptive theory. The category of knowledge is able to play its normative role precisely because it plays the causal role it does;

[24] The issue, as I lay it out here, closely tracks the current debate over moral realism. While these issues have rightly been an active topic of discussion among moral philosophers for some time now, I believe that they have not received the attention they deserve from epistemologists. For a useful anthology of papers on this issue as it arises in moral philosophy, see Geoffrey Sayre-McCord (ed.), *Essays on Moral Realism* (Cornell University Press, 1988).

[25] I have argued that knowledge has a call on us, that is, it is in the interest of creatures with beliefs and desires to attain knowledge, whether they otherwise value knowledge or not. Given my account of the source of this demand, this thereby makes for real normativity in nature. If there is some additional role that genuine normativity must play that this account somehow omits, I don't understand what that might be.

it is valuable because it provides the means by which animals may satisfy their needs, as well as their desires. One and the same category may do the work of both prescription and description.

As a naturalist, I do not find it surprising that the natural and the normative should bear this relationship to one another. More than this, I believe that the situation in epistemology may be generalized to cover other normative categories; I shall have a bit more to say about this in Ch. 6. But for now, my purpose is merely to make clear how things might stand in epistemology.

5.7 Conclusion

I have argued that epistemic evaluation finds its natural ground in our desires in a way that makes truth something we should care about, whatever else we may value. This provides us with a pragmatic account of the source of epistemic normativity, but an account that is universal and also allows truth to play a central role. Pragmatists have typically suggested that epistemic evaluation will have little to do with truth; but if I am right, it is for pragmatic reasons that truth takes on the importance it does in epistemic evaluation.

Some will, I believe, hanker after a stronger grounding for epistemic normativity, an account that would make the injunction to seek the truth not merely hypothetical, even if universal, but categorical instead. Such an account would entail that the value of truth is not merely instrumental, as I have suggested, but intrinsic, and that attaching intrinsic value to truth is not merely optional, but required. I would not be hostile to such an account, but I do not currently see any way of giving substance to it. As things stand, I believe the account of epistemic normativity I offer allows us to make sense of much of what a categorical account would provide, while simultaneously removing the mystery from epistemic norms. As far as the remainder goes, those things that a categorical account would provide that my account does not, it remains to be seen whether any real sense can be made of them.

6

What Philosophy Might Be

Gilbert Ryle, in a brief autobiographical sketch, tells the following story.

> I must have been near my middle twenties when good-humored fraternal skepticisms about the existence of my subject showed me that it really was part of my business to be able to tell people, including myself, what philosophy is . . . Anyhow, probably over-influenced by Socrates' fruitless hunt for definitions, I was soon declaring, vaguely enough but not yet modishly, that what philosophy examines is the meanings of expressions. In the discussion that followed my, I suppose, first paper to the Jowett Society, Paton asked, 'Ah, Ryle, how *exactly* do you distinguish between philosophy and lexicography?'[1]

Paton's question is, to my mind, a good one to ask, and there are analogues of Paton's question that must be faced by any attempt to explain what philosophy is. Those who favor a view of philosophy as conceptual analysis, for example, must explain, as Stephen Stich

---

[1] G. Ryle, 'Autobiographical,' in *Ryle: A Collection of Critical Essays*, ed. O. P. Wood and G. Pitcher (Doubleday, 1970), 6.

has urged,[2] how philosophy differs from cognitive anthropology. Anyone attempting to say what philosophy is should anticipate an embarrassing Paton-style question and try to answer it as squarely and convincingly as possible.

The approach I have taken to epistemology in the foregoing chapters presupposes a conception of what philosophy is or what it might be. In some ways, this conception is, I think, familiar. Following Quine, I take for granted that philosophy is continuous with the sciences. But in other respects, the conception of philosophy at work in this essay is, perhaps, not entirely familiar, and it is the goal of this chapter to say just what that conception is. I want to try to show that there is a defensible view here which, if correct, would both make sense of much of what goes on in philosophy, and, at the same time, offer some guidance as to how it might be better pursued. Finally, I want to address the Paton-style question that this conception of philosophy invites.

6.1 Philosophical kinds and natural kinds

I have been urging that knowledge is a natural kind and thus that a proper understanding of the nature of knowledge requires a certain sort of empirical investigation. It is a mistake to investigate our intuitions about knowledge or our concept of knowledge because these may be importantly incomplete or importantly mistaken or both. Indeed, we have seen that those who have attempted to come to an understanding of knowledge by way of these more traditional investigations have often lost contact with the phenomenon they seek to understand. In Ch. 3 I argued that those who have made various social practices prerequisites of knowledge are, in the end, mistaken. Although human beings are social animals, and although we do frequently engage in a social practice of giving and asking for

---

[2] See his critique of conceptual analysis in *The Fragmentation of Reason* (MIT Press, 1990), ch. 4.

reasons, thereby using and interpreting language, these social practices are not prerequisites for knowledge. And in Ch. 4, I argued that the common practice, among humans, of self-consciously considering the epistemic credentials of one's beliefs, is also not a prerequisite for knowledge. Some of these requirements turn practices that are not always epistemically valuable into preconditions for knowledge; others turn practices that are rarely engaged in, or could not be engaged in, into prerequisites for knowledge. These approaches to knowledge lose sight of the phenomenon, and thereby lose their right to be seen as viable accounts of what knowledge is.

What I have advocated instead is that the philosophical investigation of knowledge be understood as an investigation of a natural kind. My experience has been that such a suggestion is often met with incredulity. How could knowledge be investigated as if it were a natural kind? More than this, how could knowledge actually turn out to be a natural kind? I have tried to answer these questions in the foregoing chapters. Just as the category of belief is an important causal/explanatory category in psychology, the category of knowledge turns out to be an important causal/explanatory category in cognitive ethology. Just as a proper description of the psychology of animals requires that we see them as creatures having beliefs, a proper understanding of the cognitive capacities of animals requires that we see them as a means by which evolution responds to the informational demands that the environment makes on its inhabitants, and this in turn gives rise to the category of knowledge. The standards that a belief must answer to if it is to count as knowledge are not some sort of social construct; the standards for knowledge arise from the demands that nature makes on animals if they are to function in their natural environment.

This approach to epistemological questions stands in stark contrast not only to traditional approaches to epistemology, but also to the approaches of some naturalists. Alvin Goldman, for example, who has surely done more than anyone else to make the case for the importance of empirical psychology in addressing epistemological questions, has a conception of the nature of the epistemological enterprise that is strikingly traditional.[3] Goldman sees his own reliabilist account of knowledge as a product of conceptual analysis, and although on Goldman's view conceptual analysis has important empirical elements to it, his method has much in common with more traditional defenders of conceptual analysis. Goldman's view is that an account of what knowledge is must answer to our concept of knowledge, something socially constructed, and not to anything external to us. Most of the work that empirical psychology, and other empirical sciences, provide for Goldman comes in helping us to understand which processes of belief acquisition are in fact reliable; the reliability analysis itself, however, is largely a product of examining our intuitions about knowledge, considering potential examples and counterexamples.[4]

While the substance of the analysis of knowledge I have defended is largely in agreement with Goldman, the method by which it is reached is strikingly different. The category of knowledge is, on my view, an important category because it has a certain theoretical unity to it, that is, it plays a causal and explanatory role within our best current theories. Even if Goldman is right that the concept of knowledge that individuals in our society have is the concept of reliably produced true belief, this would, on my view, be of little significance. What makes this category an important one, on my view, is not that people in our society have the concept; rather, it is that this category accurately describes a feature of the world.

I have argued that this approach does not in any way deprive knowledge of its normative force. Indeed, quite the opposite. By

[3] The most recent statement of Goldman's view on this may be found in A. Goldman and J. Pust, 'Philosophical Theory and Intuitional Evidence', in M. DePaul and W. Ramsey (eds.), *Rethinking Intuition* (Rowman & Littlefield, 1998), 179–97.

[4] Largely, but not entirely. On the view defended in Goldman and Pust, 'Philosophical Theory and Intuitional Evidence', there may well be features of our concepts that are not detectable by standard philosophical means. It is for this reason that an empirical investigation of our concepts is needed to supplement the standard philosophical techniques. Nevertheless, Goldman's view is that, in practice, the standard philosophical techniques will actually take us quite far.

grounding knowledge in the world and seeing it as an evolutionary product of animals' information needs, knowledge may be properly viewed as valuable for animals, whether they independently want it or not; indeed, whether they even have the concept of knowledge or not. Such an approach thus allows us to explain why it is that the standards for knowledge are ones which matter.

I do not believe that knowledge is unique among the objects of philosophical investigation in these respects. Instead, one may view the approach to questions about knowledge taken here as illustrative of an approach that might be taken to a wide variety of philosophical questions. Many of the objects of philosophical enquiry may, like knowledge, be natural kinds, and the kind of empirical investigation practiced here may with equal profit be applied to other areas of philosophical enquiry. In addition, the kind of relationship between normative and descriptive concerns that, I have argued, is illustrated in the case of knowledge may also be characteristic of other philosophical kinds.

Consider, for example, what a number of moral realists have suggested about the nature of the right and the good. According to the kind of naturalistic approach championed by Richard Boyd,[5] David Brink,[6] Norman Daniels,[7] Richard Miller,[8] Peter Railton,[9] and Nicholas Sturgeon,[10] an account of moral properties is not arrived at by means of conceptual analysis. An understanding of moral

---

[5] Richard Boyd, 'How to be a Moral Realist', in G. Sayre-McCord (ed.), *Essays on Moral Realism* (Cornell University Press, 1988).

[6] David Brink, *Moral Realism and the Foundations of Ethics* (Cambridge University Press, 1989).

[7] Norman Daniels, 'Wide Reflective Equilibrium and Theory Acceptance in Ethics', repr. in Daniels, *Justice and Justification: Reflective Equilibrium in Theory and Practice* (Cambridge University Press, 1996).

[8] Richard Miller, *Moral Differences: Truth, Justice, and Conscience in a World of Conflict* (Princeton University Press, 1992).

[9] e.g. in 'Moral Realism', *Philosophical Review*, 95 (1986), 163–207, and 'Facts and Values', *Philosophical Topics*, 14 (1986), 5–31.

[10] e.g. in 'Moral Explanations', repr. in G. Sayre-McCord (ed.), *Essays on Moral Realism*; and 'What Difference Does Moral Realism Make?' and 'Harman on Moral Explanations of Natural Facts', both in *Southern Journal of Philosophy*, suppl. vol. 24 (1986).

properties is, in the end, an empirical investigation. Norman Daniels' discussion of wide reflective equilibrium is especially relevant here. Daniels sees an important analogy between moral enquiry and argumentation, on the one hand, and scientific enquiry and argumentation, on the other.

Consider for a moment a general argument of this form. (1) In a given area of inquiry, the methods used are successful in the sense that they produce convergence and a growth of knowledge; (2) the only plausible account of the success of these methods is that they lead us to better and better approximations to truths of the kind relevant to the inquiry; (3) therefore, we should adopt a realist account of the relevant objects of inquiry . . .

Suppose a version of such an argument for scientific realism is sound . . . Then we would be justified in claiming that certain methodological features of science, including its coherence and other theory-laden constraints on theory acceptance (e.g., parsimony, simplicity, etc.), are consensus producing *because* they are *evidential* and lead us to better approximations to the truth. I have been defending the view that coherence constraints in wide reflective equilibrium function very much like those in science. If I am right, this suggests that we may be able to piggyback a claim about objectivity in ethics onto the analogous claim that we are assuming can be made for science.[11]

The kind of argument Daniels proposes, one that is made by all the moral realists cited above, is an empirical argument. A plausible case for the realist explanation of the extent of consensus, and the extent of disagreement, must be made; and alternative explanations of the extent of consensus and disagreement must be ruled out. If such an argument can be made, not only the objectivity of ethics, but also the reality of moral properties, is thereby secured. The moral properties are not revealed by any sort of conceptual analysis, but by empirical argument.

The idea that an account of the good is thoroughly empirical is an essential part of the naturalistic brand of moral realism these philosophers defend. Thus, Boyd comments,

[11] Daniels, 'Wide Reflective Equilibrium and Theory Acceptance in Ethics', 37–8.

Knowledge of fundamental human goods and their homeostasis represents basic knowledge about human psychological and social potential. Much of this knowledge is genuinely *experimental* knowledge and the relevant experiments are ('naturally' occurring) political and social experiments whose occurrence and whose interpretation depends both on 'external' factors and upon the current state of our moral understanding. Thus, for example, we would not have been able to explore the dimensions of our needs for artistic expression and appreciation had not social and technological developments made possible cultures in which, for some classes at least, there was the leisure to produce and consume art. We would not have understood the role of political democracy in the homeostasis of the good had the conditions not arisen in which the first limited democracies developed. Only after the moral insights gained from the first democratic experiments were in hand, were we equipped to see the depth of the moral peculiarity of slavery. Only since the establishment of the first socialist societies are we even beginning to obtain the data necessary to assess the role of egalitarian social practices in fostering the good.[12]

There is thus an active research program in moral theory that treats moral properties exactly as I have treated knowledge.

The kind of empirical work in philosophy that I favor has long been a feature of discussions in the philosophy of mind. Consider, for example, Jerry Fodor's discussions of the language of thought hypothesis and the modularity of mind.[13] In each of these cases, Fodor proposes a hypothesis about the mind that arises out of empirical work in the cognitive sciences. Fodor first attempts to show that the hypothesis he favors is actually implicitly supposed in a great deal of empirical theorizing; he then seeks to show that these implicit claims are well supported by the available evidence. Fodor's recent comments about his philosophical method not only describe his own work, but that of a great many now working in the philosophy of mind.

---

[12] Boyd, 'How to be a Moral Realist', 205.
[13] See especially *The Language of Thought* (Thomas Y. Crowell, 1975) and *The Modularity of Mind* (MIT Press, 1983).

Some of the arguments I have on offer are patently philosophical; some turn on experimental and linguistic data; many are methodological; and some are just appeals to common sense. That there is no way of talking that is comfortable for all these sorts of dialectic is part of what makes doing cognitive science so hard. In the long run, I gave up; I've simply written as the topics at hand seemed to warrant. If it doesn't sound exactly like philosophy, I don't mind; as long as it doesn't sound exactly like psychology, linguistics, or AI either.[14]

Indeed, it is important to see that empirical evidence has always been a feature of discussions in the philosophy of mind. Certainly discussions of materialism and dualism, not only in contemporary work, but in Descartes and his contemporaries, involved a substantial discussion of empirical evidence.

What this work in the philosophy of mind illustrates is an attempt to understand various things about the mind, rather than our concept of the mind. Philosophers interested in questions about dualism and materialism have typically been interested in understanding what the mind is made of; they are far less interested, in this context, in questions about our concept of mind. If our concept of mind should build in various dualist presuppositions, but it should turn out that, in actual fact, the mind is entirely composed of physical stuff, then materialists win. The same is true about the issues involved in the debate about the language of thought, modularity, consciousness, and all the rest: what is important here is not our concept of mind, but the mind itself. The reason that topics in the philosophy of mind are so interesting is precisely that they are about real features of the world. We want to understand the mind because minds are salient features of human beings and other animals; they have a great deal to do with what we are. Our concept of mind, however, has changed radically over the ages, in part in response to increased scientific understanding, but also in ways that simply reflect common misunderstandings. Even when our concepts are

[14] J. Fodor, *Concepts: Where Cognitive Science Went Wrong* (Oxford University Press, 1998), p. viii.

shaped by scientific advances, they do not typically keep pace with the best currently available theories. If we want to understand the mind, then we would be well advised to look to our best current theories rather than the concepts we have prior to such theoretical engagement. And this is what one sees in much of the current work in this area. What I have been advocating in this essay is that this same approach, an approach that has been used to such great effect in the philosophy of mind, be brought to work in epistemology as well.

The idea that philosophy should be thought of as an investigation of various features of the world is thus a thought that is not entirely alien to current philosophical practice. While epistemology has not typically been thought of or practiced in this way, this kind of approach to philosophical questions is well represented in the current philosophical literature, and it is one that may be brought to epistemology with some real benefit.

6.2 *Paton's embarrassing question*

The question that Paton asked Ryle is a good one, not because the mere asking of the question shows Ryle's view of philosophy to be mistaken; it doesn't. Rather, Paton's question is a good one because it forces Ryle and those who share his conception of philosophy to articulate more clearly their view of what philosophy is and what it might be. Better still, Paton's question may be brought to bear on any conception of philosophy, to similar effect.

The view of philosophy I have been urging here is one that sees philosophy as a thoroughly empirical discipline. And this invites an embarrassing series of questions, starting with what I will now call 'Paton's question': 'Ah, Kornblith, how *exactly* do you distinguish between philosophy and the special sciences?' Does epistemology, on this view, become a branch of cognitive ethology? And how is it that philosophers are in a position to answer philosophical questions, given this conception of what philosophy is? Surely nothing in the way philosophers are trained gives us any reason to think that they are well qualified to answer the kinds of questions that, on the view defended here, philosophical questions turn out to be.[15]

I am quite sure that I am not in a position to say *exactly* how philosophy differs from the special sciences; certainly not in a way that would have satisfied H. J. Paton. I can, however, say something in response to Paton's question, something which will, I hope, point the way to a more fully satisfying answer. Along with W. V. Quine, I see philosophy as continuous with the sciences. And along with Wilfrid Sellars, I believe that, 'The aim of philosophy, abstractly formulated, is to understand how things in the broadest possible sense of the term hang together in the broadest possible sense of the term.'[16] The Quinean view, however, is precisely what raises Paton's question, and it must be acknowledged that what Sellars says does not do a great deal to answer it. While philosophy does seem to concern itself, at times, with questions that are broader or more abstract than those that are to be found in the special sciences, and while it may rightly be said that these differences seem to be nothing more than a matter of degree, with the boundaries between philosophy and the sciences accordingly blurry, it would be nice to have a bit more to say here about what is distinctive about philosophy.

The various questions with which philosophy has traditionally concerned itself are often ones that the special sciences do not directly address. Many philosophical questions deal with normative issues, although certainly not all do. It is not clear to me whether there is any one thing that all philosophical questions have in common, other than their common history. Certainly many of the traditional views about what makes a problem uniquely philosophical

---

[15] This last point has been presented in a particularly pointed form by Richard Fumerton in his 'Skepticism and Naturalistic Epistemology', *Midwest Studies in Philosophy*, 19 (1994), 321–40, and 'A Priori Philosophy after an A Posteriori Turn', *Midwest Studies in Philosophy*, 23 (1999), 21–33.

[16] Wilfrid Sellars, 'Philosophy and the Scientific Image of Man', in his *Science, Perception and Reality* (Routledge & Kegan Paul, 1963), 1.

are ones that I am committed to rejecting. Clearly, I do not accept the view that what is distinctive of philosophical questions is that they may be approached a priori. I do, however, believe that many of the questions that philosophers have traditionally addressed are indeed legitimate questions, and that the methods that have traditionally been used to answer these questions—various a priori methods—are not likely to bear fruit. So, whatever philosophical questions may be, I believe that they deserve answers, and that empirical methods are the ones that are most likely to be successful in generating those answers.

In the case of epistemology, I do not see it as nothing more than a branch of cognitive ethology. While I have argued that knowledge turns out to be a category that is generated by ethological concerns, many of the concerns that are properly philosophical are ones that do not arise within ethology. Ethologists have little interest, qua ethologists, in normative questions about belief, and they have little interest, qua ethologists, in questions about the relationship between the normative and the descriptive dimensions of knowledge. If the view I have defended here is correct, then work in ethology turns out to be importantly relevant in *answering* these questions, but the questions themselves do not arise within ethology proper. This does not make them any less legitimate.

I believe that this is often true of philosophical issues: the concerns that raise them do not arise from within any of the special sciences, even though the special sciences turn out to be relevant in providing the answers. Many philosophical questions cut across several different sciences; they do not arise within any single science, and a proper answer to these questions requires a multidisciplinary response. I do not have any views about what it is that distinguishes the philosophical multidisciplinary problems from other non-philosophical multidisciplinary problems. But there certainly may be a hidden unity here waiting to be discovered.

I thus have little light to shed on the question of what it is that makes a problem philosophical, even if I do have views about proper method in philosophy. But my views about method do raise a question about the competence of philosophers to address philosophical problems. This question has been put most clearly by Richard Fumerton: 'if paradigm naturalist/externalist metaepistemologies are correct, then normative epistemology is an inappropriate subject matter for philosophy. Philosophers as they are presently trained have no special *philosophical* expertise . . .'[17] Fumerton's point here is not just a point about normative epistemology, for if Fumerton is right about that, then the point is perfectly general: if philosophy is what naturalists say it is, then philosophers, as they are presently trained, simply are not competent to address philosophical questions. Indeed, Fumerton himself goes on to apply his point to work in normative ethics:

although we live in an age of philosophical toleration, I urge us to take seriously the positivists' disparaging remarks about normative ethics as a field of philosophy . . . I wouldn't trust a philosopher, not even a philosopher who works a great deal in applied ethics. Philosophers tend to lead lives that are far too sheltered from the realities of life. The people with the best empirical evidence to settle ethical disputes that arise within medicine, business, agriculture, warfare, and so on are doctors, economists, psychologists, sociologists, soldiers, and generally people who exhibit good common sense.[18]

Fumerton thus argues that if naturalism is correct, then philosophy must be taken away from philosophers. Indeed, although Fumerton rejects naturalism, he endorses the conclusion that normative ethics should, in fact, be taken away from philosophers.

Fumerton's ideas of what philosophy is, and what current philosophical training is, are quite different from mine. Certainly it is possible to get an advanced degree in philosophy, and to have a successful career as a professional philosopher, without ever taking a course in any of the special sciences, and, indeed, without any

---

[17] Fumerton, 'Skepticism and Naturalistic Epistemology', 333.
[18] Fumerton, 'A Priori Philosophy after an A Posteriori Turn', 31.

interest in, or knowledge of, anything empirical. The question is whether this is a good thing, and whether this is the sort of training that philosophers ought to have if they are to address successfully the questions with which they have a professional concern. Just as some philosophers have no interest in things empirical, there are also philosophers who have extensive training in empirical matters that are relevant to their philosophical concerns. The ranks of philosophers of mind who have done extensive work in the cognitive sciences is increasing by the day. The ranks of philosophers of science who have advanced training in one or more of the sciences is similarly increasing. Brand Blanshard's famous remark—'Some people know more and more about less and less until they know everything about nothing. These are philosophers'—while it was always a caricature of the field, is even further from the truth today than it was in the heyday of philosophical analysis. There are many fields in philosophy, as it is practiced today, where one simply is not competent by current professional standards unless one has a great deal of empirical understanding. The extent to which graduate students are urged to gain some high-level understanding of related empirical fields suggests that Fumerton's view of philosophical training is, perhaps, a bit narrow. This trend toward greater empirical engagement in philosophical training seems to me a good thing, and very much the sort of thing that is needed if my account of philosophical method is even close to correct.

Fumerton says that he would not trust a philosopher on normative matters because philosophers lead lives that are too 'sheltered from the realities of life'. Those who are best informed about the relevant empirical issues that are crucial to deciding normative questions are not philosophers, but rather 'doctors, economists, psychologists, sociologists, soldiers, and generally people who exhibit good common sense'. But while these individuals are typically better informed about relevant empirical matters than the philosophers who make normative questions their concern, Fumerton backs away from just handing over the normative questions to these people as well: 'Of course the people with the best empirical evidence don't necessarily have the kind of theoretical knowledge that would enable them to put their empirical knowledge to the best use.'[19] More than this, Fumerton suggests that it might be a 'good idea' for these individuals to have some training in what he calls 'theoretical ethics'.[20] But this is just to acknowledge that there are certain sorts of questions, the ones philosophers are frequently concerned with, that may not engage those who are often most directly acquainted with relevant empirical information. More than this, what is required in order to solve these questions is a serious engagement with the issues together with a thorough understanding of the relevant empirical matters. As things stand, doctors, economists, psychologists, sociologists, soldiers, and so on often lack the interest, and certain aspects of the training, to engage these questions profitably. And, as Fumerton would surely agree, narrowly trained philosophers lack an important piece of what is required here as well. Fumerton is also surely right that certain sorts of lifestyles—in particular, those that shelter one from personal engagement with situations in which certain important moral issues arise—make one less well-suited to addressing those normative issues. On the question of normative ethics then, it sounds as if Fumerton's disagreement with the position defended here amounts to little more than an unwillingness to call people philosophers if they have a great deal of empirical understanding informed, in part, by a life that is morally engaged. My view is simply that these people are in the best position to do philosophy.

The very training which Fumerton sees as overly narrow for addressing normative concerns—the kind of training that he regards as properly philosophical—is, to my mind, no better suited for other philosophical investigations than it is for normative ethics. Theorizing about knowledge is enriched by engagement with the empirical literature in cognitive science, cognitive ethology, and the

---

[19] Ibid.   [20] Ibid.

history of science. One is better able to theorize about knowledge if one has a real understanding of the phenomenon itself, and this requires some engagement with the empirical literature on a variety of subjects. Acquiring such empirical understanding does not, on my view, deprive one of one's standing as a philosopher; it is, to my mind, what is required if one is best to achieve the understanding that is a philosopher's goal.

Fumerton's view of what philosophy is has a purity to it which mine does not. But this view of philosophy first forces one to give up on a number of traditional philosophical topics, and arguably leaves philosophy less well-suited to address the rest. By giving up on this conception of the purity of philosophy, we may both enrich our conception of what philosophy is and thereby leave it better prepared to address the questions that we all agree deserve responsible answers.

It is also worth pointing out that this conception of philosophy sits well with the practice of philosophy throughout most of its history. The great philosophers of the past were not narrowly trained specialists, ignorant of relevant empirical information. Those who wrote about epistemology and metaphysics were often well-informed about the best science of their day; quite a number of them were able scientists in their own right. Many philosophers who wrote about issues in moral philosophy, and on broader social and political questions, were very far from leading the sheltered lives that Fumerton rightly sees as inimical to proper engagement with normative concerns. Philosophy informed in these ways has always been the best our field has to offer. We should not narrow our conception of philosophy in a way that cuts it off from the very source of its depth and value.

6.3 Conclusion

A view of philosophy as empirically informed does not take philosophy away from philosophers, although it does suggest ways in which the training of philosophers may, at times, have been overly narrow. Philosophy may properly be viewed as empirically informed theory construction without, at the same time, turning it into a series of chapters within the special sciences.

BIBLIOGRAPHY

ACHINSTEIN, PETER, *The Concept of Evidence* (Oxford University Press, 1983).

ALCOCK, JOHN, *Animal Behavior: An Evolutionary Approach* (Sinauer Associates, 1975).

ALLEN, COLIN, 'Mental Content', *British Journal for the Philosophy of Science*, 43 (1992), 537–53.

—— 'Animal Pain', manuscript.

ALLEN, COLIN, and BEKOFF, MARC, *Species of Mind: The Philosophy and Biology of Cognitive Ethology* (MIT Press, 1997).

ALLEN, COLIN, BEKOFF, MARK, and LAUDER, GEORGE (eds), *Nature's Purposes: Analyses of Function and Design in Biology* (MIT Press, 1998).

ASTINGTON, JANET WILDE, *The Child's Discovery of the Mind* (Harvard University Press, 1993).

AYER, A. J., *The Concept of a Person and Other Essays* (Macmillan, 1964).

BALDA, R. P., PEPPERBERG, I. M., and KAMIL, A. C. (eds), *Animal Cognition in Nature: The Convergence of Psychology and Biology in Laboratory and Field* (Academic Press, 1998).

BARKOW, JEROME H., COSMIDES, LEDA, and TOOBY, JOHN (eds), *The Adapted Mind: Evolutionary Psychology and the Generation of Culture* (Oxford University Press, 1992).

BEALER, GEORGE, 'The Philosophical Limits of Scientific Essentialism', *Philosophical Perspectives*, 1 (1987), 289–365.

—— 'The Incoherence of Empiricism', in S. Wagner and R. Warner (eds), *Naturalism: A Critical Appraisal* (Notre Dame University Press, 1993), 163–96.

—— 'Intuition and the Autonomy of Philosophy', in M. DePaul and W. Ramsey (eds) (1998), 201–39.

BEKOFF, MARC, and JAMIESON, DALE (eds), *Interpretation and Explanation in the Study of Animal Behavior*, i. *Interpretation, Intentionality, and Communication* (Westview, 1990).

BENDER, JOHN (ed), *The Current State of the Coherence Theory: Critical Essays on the Epistemic Theories of Keith Lehrer and Laurence BonJour, with Replies* (Kluwer, 1989).

BERMÚDEZ, JOSÉ LUIS, *The Paradox of Self-Consciousness*, MIT Press, 1998.

BONJOUR, LAURENCE, *The Structure of Empirical Knowledge* (Harvard University Press, 1985).

—— 'Replies and Clarifications', in Bender (ed) (1989), 276–92.

—— 'Against Naturalistic Epistemology', *Midwest Studies in Philosophy*, 19 (1994), 283–300.

—— 'The Dialectic of Foundationalism and Coherentism', in J. Greco and E. Sosa (eds) (1999), 117–42.

—— 'Toward a Defense of Empirical Foundationalism', in Michael DePaul (ed), *Resurrecting Old-Fashioned Foundationalism* (Rowman & Littlefield, 2001), 21–38.

BOYD, RICHARD, 'How to Be a Moral Realist', in Geoffrey Sayre-McCord (ed), *Essays on Moral Realism* (Cornell University Press, 1988), 181–228.

BRANDOM, ROBERT, *Making It Explicit: Reasoning, Representing and Discursive Commitment* (Harvard University Press, 1994).

—— 'Insights and Blindspots of Reliabilism', *Monist*, 81 (1998), 371–92.

—— *Articulating Reasons: An Introduction to Inferentialism* (Harvard University Press, 2000).

BRINK, DAVID, *Moral Realism and the Foundations of Ethics* (Cambridge University Press, 1989).

BUTCHVAROV, PANAYOT, *The Concept of Knowledge* (Northwestern University Press, 1970).

CAREY, SUSAN, and XU, FEI, 'Infants' Knowledge of Objects: Beyond Object Files and Object Tracking', *Cognition*, 40 (2001), 1–35.

CHENEY, DOROTHY, and SEYFARTH, ROBERT, *How Monkeys See the World* (University of Chicago Press, 1990).

CHERNIAK, CHRISTOPHER, 'Computational Complexity and the Universal Acceptance of Logic', *Journal of Philosophy*, 81 (1984), 739–58.

—— *Minimal Rationality* (MIT Press, 1986).

CHISHOLM, RODERICK, *Theory of Knowledge*, 2nd edn. (Prentice-Hall, 1977).

Cummins, Denise Dellarosa, and Allen, Colin (eds), *The Evolution of Mind* (Oxford University Press, 1998).

Daniels, Norman, 'Wide Reflective Equilibrium and Theory Acceptance in Ethics', repr. in *Justice and Justification: Reflective Equilibrium in Theory and Practice* (Cambridge University Press, 1996).

Davidson, Donald, *Inquiries into Truth and Interpretation* (Oxford University Press, 1984).

—— 'Reply to Simon J. Evnine', in Hahn (ed) (1999), 305–10.

Dennett, Daniel, *Content and Consciousness* (Routledge & Kegan Paul, 1969).

—— *Brainstorms* (Bradford Books, 1978).

—— *The Intentional Stance* (MIT Press, 1987).

DePaul, Michael, and Ramsey, William (eds), *Rethinking Intuition: The Psychology of Intuition and Its Role in Philosophical Inquiry* (Rowman & Littlefield, 1998).

Descartes, René, *The Philosophical Works of Descartes*, ed. E. S. Haldane and G. R. T. Ross (2 vols; Cambridge University Press, 1931).

Devitt, Michael, 'The Methodology of Naturalistic Semantics', *Journal of Philosophy*, 91 (1994), 545–72.

Dretske, Fred, 'Two Conceptions of Knowledge: Rational vs. Reliable Belief', *Grazer Philosophische Studien*, 4 (1991), 15–30.

Elgin, Catherine, 'The Epistemic Efficacy of Stupidity', *Synthese*, 74 (1988), 297–311.

Evnine, Simon, 'On the Way to Language', in Hahn (ed) (1999), 289–304.

Field, Hartry, 'Realism and Relativism', *Journal of Philosophy*, 79 (1982), 553–67.

Fodor, Jerry, *The Language of Thought* (Thomas Y. Crowell, 1975).

—— 'Special Sciences', in *Representations: Philosophical Essays on the Foundations of Cognitive Science* (MIT Press, 1981).

—— *The Modularity of Mind* (MIT Press, 1983).

—— 'Why Paramecia Don't Have Mental Representations', *Midwest Studies in Philosophy*, 10 (1986), 3–23.

—— *Concepts: Where Cognitive Science Went Wrong* (Oxford University Press, 1998).

—— *The Mind Doesn't Work that Way: The Scope and Limits of Computational Psychology* (MIT Press, 2000).

Fogelin, Robert, *Pyrrhonian Reflections on Knowledge and Justification* (Oxford University Press, 1994).

FUMERTON, RICHARD, 'Skepticism and Naturalistic Epistemology', *Midwest Studies in Philosophy*, 19 (1994), 321–40.

—— 'A Priori Philosophy after an A Posteriori Turn', *Midwest Studies in Philosophy*, 23 (1999), 21–33.

GIBBARD, ALLAN, 'Thoughts, Norms and Discursive Practice: Commentary on Robert Brandom, *Making It Explicit*', *Philosophy and Phenomenological Research*, 56 (1996), 699–717.

GODFREY-SMITH, PETER, *Complexity and the Function of Mind in Nature* (Cambridge University Press, 1998).

GOLDMAN, ALVIN, *Epistemology and Cognition* (Harvard University Press, 1986).

—— 'Psychology and Philosophical Analysis', *Proceedings of the Aristotelian Society*, 89 (1988), 195–209.

—— *Liaisons: Philosophy Meets the Cognitive and Social Sciences* (MIT Press, 1992).

GOLDMAN, ALVIN, and PUST, JOEL, 'Philosophical Theory and Intuitional Evidence', in DePaul and Ramsey (eds) (1998).

GOPNIK, ALISON, and MELTZOFF, ANDREW, *Words, Thoughts, and Theories* (MIT Press, 1997).

GOULD, STEPHEN JAY, and LEWONTIN, RICHARD, 'The Spandrels of San Marcos and the Panglossian Paradigm: A Critique of the Adaptationist Programme', *Proceedings of the Royal Society of London*, 205 (1978), 281–8.

GOULD, STEPHEN JAY, and VRBA, ELISABETH, 'Exaptation—A Missing Term in the Science of Form', *Paleobiology*, 8 (1982), 4–15.

GRECO, JOHN, and SOSA, ERNEST, *The Blackwell Guide to Epistemology* (Blackwell, 1999).

GRIFFIN, DONALD, *The Question of Animal Awareness*, 2nd edn. (Rockefeller University Press, 1981).

—— *Animal Thinking* (Harvard University Press, 1984).

—— *Animal Minds* (University of Chicago Press, 1992).

HAHN, LEWIS (ed), *The Philosophy of Donald Davidson* (Open Court, 1999).

HAHN, LEWIS, and SCHILLP, PAUL (eds), *The Philosophy of W. V. Quine* (Open Court, 1986).

HART, H. L. A., *The Concept of Law* (Oxford University Press, 1961).

HAUGELAND, JOHN, *Having Thought: Essays in the Metaphysics of Mind* (Harvard University Press, 1998).

HAUSER, MARC, *The Evolution of Communication* (MIT Press, 1996).

HAUSER, MARC, *Wild Minds: What Animals Really Think* (Henry Holt, 2000).

HEINRICH, BERND, *Mind of the Raven: Investigations and Adventures with Wolf-Birds* (Harper Collins, 1999).

HERMAN, LOUIS, and MORREL-SAMUELS, PALMER, 'Knowledge Acquisition and Asymmetry Between Language Comprehension and Production: Dolphins and Apes as General Models for Animals', in M. Bekoff and D. Jamieson (eds) (1990), 283–312.

HOBSON, R. PETER, 'On Not Understanding Minds', *Monographs of the Society for Research in Child Development*, 61 (1996), 153–60.

HORGAN, TERRY, 'The Austere Ideology of Folk Psychology', *Mind and Language*, 8 (1993), 282–97.

HORGAN, TERRY, and GRAHAM, GEORGE, 'Southern Fundamentalism and the End of Philosophy', *Philosophical Issues*, 5 (1994), 219–47.

JACKSON, FRANK, *From Metaphysics to Ethics: A Defense of Conceptual Analysis* (Oxford University Press, 1998).

KAHNEMAN, DANIEL, SLOVIC, PAUL, and TVERSKY, AMOS (eds), *Judgment under Uncertainty: Heuristics and Biases* (Cambridge University Press, 1982).

KAPLAN, MARK, 'Epistemology Denatured', *Midwest Studies in Philosophy*, 19 (1994), 350–65.

KORNBLITH, HILARY, 'Justified Belief and Epistemically Responsible Action', *Philosophical Review*, 92 (1983), 33–48.

—— 'Ever Since Descartes', *Monist*, 68 (1985), 264–76.

—— 'Naturalizing Rationality', in N. Garver and P. Hare (eds), *Naturalism and Rationality* (Prometheus Books), 115–33.

—— 'Introspection and Misdirection', *Australasian Journal of Philosophy*, 67 (1989), 410–22.

—— 'The Unattainability of Coherence', in J. Bender (ed), *The Current State of the Coherence Theory* (Kluwer, 1989), 207–14.

—— 'Epistemic Normativity', *Synthèse*, 94 (1993), 357–76.

—— *Inductive Inference and Its Natural Ground* (MIT Press, 1993).

—— 'A Conservative Approach to Social Epistemology', in Fred Schmitt (ed), *Socializing Epistemology* (Rowman & Littlefield, 1994), 93–110.

—— 'Naturalistic Epistemology and Its Critics', *Philosophical Topics*, 23 (1995), 237–55.

—— 'The Role of Intuition in Philosophical Inquiry', in M. DePaul and W. Ramsey (eds) (1998), 129–41.

—— 'Knowledge in Humans and Other Animals', *Philosophical Perspectives*, 13 (1999), 327–46.

—— 'Sosa on Human and Animal Knowledge', in J. Greco (ed), *Sosa and His Critics* (Blackwell, forthcoming).

LEHRER, KEITH, *Meta-Mind* (Oxford University Press, 1990).

—— 'Discursive Knowledge', *Philosophy and Phenomenological Research*, 60 (2000), 637–53.

LEWIS, DAVID, *Philosophical Papers* (2 vols; Oxford University Press, 1983; 1986).

LEWONTIN, RICHARD, 'The Evolution of Cognition', in D. Osherson and E. Smith (eds) (1990).

LORD, C., ROSS, L., and LEPPER, M., 'Biased Assimilation and Attitude Polarization: The Effects of Prior Theories on Subsequently Considered Evidence', *Journal of Personality and Social Psychology*, 34 (1979).

LYCAN, WILLIAM, ' "Is" and "Ought" in Cognitive Science', *Behavioral and Brain Sciences*, 4 (1981), 344–5.

—— *Judgment and Justification* (Cambridge University Press, 1988).

MARLER, PETER, KARKAHIAN, STEPHEN, and GYGER, MARCEL, 'Do Animals Have the Option of Withholding Signals When Communication is Inappropriate? The Audience Effect', in C. Ristau (ed) (1991), 187–208.

MCGINN, COLIN, 'The Concept of Knowledge', *Midwest Studies in Philosophy*, 9 (1984), 529–54.

MILLER, GEORGE, 'The Magical Number Seven Plus or Minus Two: Some Limits on Our Capacity for Processing Information', in *The Psychology of Communication* (Basic Books, 1967).

MILLER, RICHARD W., *Moral Differences: Truth, Justice, and Conscience in a World of Conflict* (Princeton University Press, 1992).

MILLIKAN, RUTH, *Language, Thought and Other Biological Categories* (MIT Press, 1984).

—— *White Queen Psychology and Other Essays for Alice* (MIT Press, 1993).

—— *On Clear and Confused Ideas: An Essay about Substance Concepts* (Cambridge University Press, 2000).

NAGEL, THOMAS, *The View from Nowhere* (Oxford University Press, 1986).

NISBETT, RICHARD, and ROSS, LEE, *Human Inference: Strategies and Shortcomings of Social Judgment* (Prentice-Hall, 1980).

NOZICK, ROBERT, *Philosophical Explanations* (Harvard University Press, 1981).

OSHERSON, DANIEL, and SMITH, EDWARD (eds), *Thinking: An Invitation to Cognitive Science* (MIT Press, 1990), iii.

PEPPERBERG, IRENE, *The Alex Studies: Cognitive and Communicative Abilities of Grey Parrots* (Harvard University Press, 1999).

PEREBOOM, DERK, and KORNBLITH, HILARY, 'The Metaphysics of Irreducibility', *Philosophical Studies*, 63 (1991), 131–51.

PINKER, STEVEN, *How the Mind Works* (W. W. Norton, 1997).

PLOTKIN, HENRY, *Darwin Machines and the Nature of Knowledge* (Harvard University Press, 1994).

POVINELLI, DANIEL, *Folk Physics for Apes: The Chimpanzee's Theory of How the World Works* (Oxford University Press, 2000).

POVINELLI, DANIEL, and EDDY, TIMOTHY, 'What Young Chimpanzees Know about Seeing', *Monographs of the Society for Research in Child Development*, 61 (1996), 1–152.

PUTNAM, HILARY, 'Brains and Behavior', in *Mind, Language and Reality: Philosophical Papers* (Cambridge University Press, 1975), ii. 325–41.

QUINE, W. V. O., *Ontological Relativity and Other Essays* (Columbia University Press, 1969).

—— 'Reply to Morton White', in Lewis Hahn and Paul Schilpp (eds) (1986), 663–5.

RAILTON, PETER, 'Moral Realism', *Philosophical Review*, 95 (1986), 163–207.

—— 'Facts and Values', *Philosophical Topics*, 14 (1986), 5–31.

RISTAU, CAROLYN (ed), *Cognitive Ethology: The Minds of Other Animals: Essays in Honor of Donald R. Griffin* (Lawrence Erlbaum, 1991).

—— 'Aspects of the Cognitive Ethology of an Injury-Feigning Bird, the Piping Plover', in Ristau (ed) (1991).

RYLE, GILBERT, *The Concept of Mind* (Barnes & Noble, 1949).

—— 'Autobiographical', in *Ryle: A Collection of Critical Essays*, ed. O. P. Wood and G. Pitcher (Doubleday, 1970).

SAYRE-MCCORD, GEOFFREY (ed), *Essays on Moral Realism* (Cornell University Press, 1988).

SCHOLL, BRIAN J., and LESLIE, ALAN M., 'Explaining the Infant's Object Concept: Beyond the Perception/Cognition Dichotomy', in E. LePore and Z. Pylyshyn (eds), *What Is Cognitive Science?* (Blackwell, 1999), 26–73.

SELLARS, WILFRID, 'Philosophy and the Scientific Image of Man', in *Science, Perception and Reality* (Routledge & Kegan Paul, 1963).

SHETTLEWORTH, SARA, *Cognition, Evolution and Behavior* (Oxford University Press, 1998).

SHOEMAKER, SYDNEY, *The First-Person Perspective and Other Essays* (Cambridge University Press, 1996).

SIEGEL, HARVEY, 'Empirical Psychology, Naturalized Epistemology and First Philosophy', *Philosophy of Science*, 51 (1984), 667–76.

SOBER, ELLIOTT, *Philosophy of Biology*, 2nd edn. (Westview, 2000).

SORABJI, RICHARD, *Animal Minds and Human Morals: The Origins of the Western Debate* (Cornell University Press, 1993).

SOSA, ERNEST, *Knowledge in Perspective: Selected Essays in Epistemology* (Cambridge University Press, 1991).

—— 'Reflective Knowledge in the Best Circles', *Journal of Philosophy*, 94 (1997), 410–30.

STEIN, EDWARD, *Without Good Reason: The Rationality Debate in Philosophy and Cognitive Science* (Oxford University Press, 1996).

STICH, STEPHEN, *The Fragmentation of Reason* (MIT Press, 1990).

STURGEON, NICHOLAS, 'Moral Explanations', 1985; repr. in G. Sayre-McCord (ed) (1988).

—— 'Harman on Moral Explanations of Natural Facts', *Southern Journal of Philosophy*, suppl. vol. 24 (1986).

—— 'What Difference Does Moral Realism Make?', *Southern Journal of Philosophy*, suppl. vol. 24 (1986).

TOMASELLO, MICHAEL, 'Chimpanzee Social Cognition', *Monographs of the Society for Research in Child Development*, 61 (1996), 161–73.

TOMASELLO, MICHAEL, and CALL, JOSEP, *Primate Cognition* (Oxford University Press, 1997).

TVERSKY, AMOS, and KAHNEMAN, DANIEL, 'Judgment under Uncertainty: Heuristics and Biases', repr. in Kahneman, Slovic, and Tversky (eds) (1982).

VAUCLAIR, JACQUES, *Animal Cognition: An Introduction to Modern Comparative Psychology* (Harvard University Press, 1996).

WASON, PETER, 'On the Failure to Eliminate Hypotheses in a Conceptual Task', *Quarterly Journal of Experimental Psychology*, 12 (1960), 129–40.

WASON, PETER, and JOHNSON-LAIRD, PHILIP, *Psychology of Reasoning: Structure and Content* (Harvard University Press, 1972).

WILLIAMS, G. C., *Adaptation and Natural Selection* (Princeton University Press, 1966).

WILLIAMS, MICHAEL, *Unnatural Doubt: Epistemological Realism and the Basis of Scepticism* (Princeton University Press, 1996).

—— *Groundless Belief: An Essay on the Possibility of Epistemology*, 2nd edn. (Princeton University Press, 1999).

WILLIAMS, MICHAEL, 'Dretske on Epistemic Entitlement', *Philosophy and Phenomenological Research*, 60 (2000), 607–12.

—— *Problems of Knowledge: A Critical Introduction to Philosophical Epistemology* (Oxford University Press, 2001).

WITTGENSTEIN, LUDWIG, *Philosophical Investigations*, 3rd edn. (Macmillan, 1953).

INDEX